MY LIFE AND BOOKS

S. M. Houghton

MY LIFE AND BOOKS

The Reminiscences of
S. M. HOUGHTON

THE BANNER OF TRUTH TRUST

THE BANNER OF TRUTH TRUST
3 Murrayfield Road, Edinburgh EH12 6EL
PO Box 621, Carlisle, Pennsylvania 17013, USA

★

© The Banner of Truth Trust 1988
First published 1988
ISBN 0 85151 537 1

★

Typeset in 10½/12pt Linotron Plantin
at The Spartan Press Ltd, Lymington, Hants
and printed and bound in Great Britain
at the University Printing House, Oxford

TO

ANDREW, NICHOLAS, JOANNA, PAUL,
PETER, JANET, SIMON and THOMAS

CONTENTS

PUBLISHER'S PREFACE

The first nine chapters of this book were written for *The Banner of Truth* magazine between February 1973 and January 1974, and the tenth for the June issue of 1987, which was the month of the author's death. There has been a widespread wish that they should now be republished in this more accessible and permanent form.

These pages reveal a little of the great debt which we owe as publishers to S. M. Houghton. For some 30 years he was an outstanding helper in all the work of the Banner of Truth Trust, and his professional aid led to the enrichment of thousands around the world.

We who knew and loved him are the spiritually poorer for his absence. We thank God for him and trust that the testimony of these pages may be used to help in the preparation of others who will serve Christ and His cause with similar faithfulness and fruitfulness in days to come.

March 1988

1: *First Interests*

Having been invited to write in autobiographical strain and to weave some mention of the influence of books upon me into my narrative, I set my mind accordingly to reflect upon happenings in my youth, at the outset chiefly to the second decade of the present century, when, alas, decadence in respect of Christian doctrine had set in on an alarming scale, and the so-called Higher Criticism had swept like a whirlwind through not a few branches of the church. Not that I was aware of the decadence or of the departure from fundamental doctrine; on the contrary, I believed that the church to which I was linked from my birth and 'christening' was within reach of perfection. In the national scene my years of adolescence were spent under the shadow of war, and ere the First World War ended it had caught me in its toils.

My ancestry, maternal and paternal, was ardently Methodist.[1] John Wesley and his equally illustrious brother Charles were, in a sense, a part of my heritage. Their sermons, their hymns, their witness to Christ, their legacy to the Christian church, were held in the highest esteem. I well remember my father's father (born, I suppose, as also was my mother's father, in or about

[1]His parents were Joseph and Edith (*née* Edge) Houghton. Sidney Maurice Houghton was born at their home in Zechariah Street, Salford (a western suburb of Manchester), Lancashire, on November 20, 1899. He had two brothers, William who died in 1908 at the age of seven, and Ernest who died as a babe in 1911. His sisters, Elsie and Marjorie, lived to 1958 and 1987 respectively.

1840), in the early years of the century as he lay upon what proved to be his death-bed, saying to me, 'Do all you can for the Lord Jesus'. I cherish the remembrance, for although, as I look back, I feel that a Christian word in a different strain would have been more fitted to my childish ignorance and my spiritual state then, there is thankfulness in my heart that my ancestry was keyed to the Christian pattern. Correspondingly, on the material side, I well recollect the occasion when, the contents of the home of my grandfather being dispersed, I was presented with a property which, as I was given to understand, had once belonged to my grandmother's father. It consisted of the six volumes of sermons, completely typical of English Puritanism, published under the title of *Morning Exercises* (preached at St Giles in the Fields, Cripplegate, and also at Southwark) between 1660 and 1690. The Prefaces to the volumes are, in turn, by Thomas Case, Nathanael Vincent, and Samuel Annesley, the last-named being the father of the renowned Susannah, mother of the Wesley brothers. One of the books is devoted in its entirety of 883 quarto pages to sermons 'against Popery', the first being by Matthew Poole. The preaching took place at a very early hour of the day, in reference to which fact the first of the Prefaces, that by Thomas Case, opens thus delightfully:

It is no small advantage to the holy life, to begin the day with God. The saints are wont to leave their hearts with him over night, that they may find them with him in the morning; 'when I awake I am still with Thee', saith holy David (*Psalm 139:18*). Before earthly things break in upon us, and we receive impressions from abroad, 'tis good to season the heart with thoughts of God, and to consecrate the early and virgin operations of the mind, before they are prostituted to baser objects.

The names of the various preachers – William Bates, John Owen, Thomas Manton, Edmund Calamy, Thomas Adams, and not a few others – are in my volumes, not printed against their sermons, but written in a clear hand by John Ballantyne who appears to have been their first owner. An eighteenth-century owner was a certain T. Robinson, and maybe the first nineteenth-century owner was my own great-grandfather. In booksellers' parlance they would be described as 'Contents good, spines poor and amateurishly repaired'. To me, as inherited treasures, they are wonderfully valuable. They came to me as a gift from the Lord, for by the time I received them I had known the divine call by grace, and relations who lacked my new-found interest in the Puritans rightly judged that, theologically, the books and I were akin. I was happy to think that, three generations before my arrival in the world, such books found lodging in the home, and I trust also in the hearts, of my forbears.

I had an early liking for books, inherited chiefly from my father who was himself a book-lover and whose modest library, occupying as it did one entire wall of the 'middle room' (for such the dining room was termed), drew out my childish interest; and I would add, by way of anticipation only, that it contained a copy of Gurnall's *Christian in Complete Armour*. It was not the case that, in the days of my unregeneracy, I explored the library, for the books were mostly religious, if not severely theological, and my early interests ran in different channels. Each week, as a teenager, I visited the Carnegie, the library of the Lancashire borough in which I was brought up.[2] My mother tried to exercise a measure of oversight lest she

[2] Andrew Carnegie was a native of Dunfermline. Having made a fortune amounting to at least 500 million dollars out of American steel, he devoted much of it in later life to philanthropic purposes, including the building and endowing of libraries in many parts of the world. He died in 1919.

should find my blood curdled, and lest the dreams of youth should be turned into nightmares, of which there was a danger. On one occasion I remember taking a book home entitled *Uncanny Tales* written by an American novelist. My mother noted, as I entered the home, that I tried to keep the book concealed, and asked me its title. I mystified her by pronouncing 'uncanny' in deliberately non-dictionary fashion, and as hurriedly as possible got the volume into my bedroom. I can only say that far too much of my time was spent in those days over worthless fiction. My conversion resulted in a lifelong reaction against that type of literature. In later life I once endeavoured to further my 'education' by reading a work of fiction – to be precise, *The Forsyte Saga* by John Galsworthy – but found it quite impossible to get further than the opening pages.

Of Scripture I knew little and understood less. At the age of seven I was entered for a Scripture examination, quite a common event in Methodist circles, and obtained a first-class certificate, but the fact is, that I did not possess a Bible of my own until I reached the age of seventeen or eighteen, and somewhat strangely, I seemed to have had no desire for one. My knowledge of the Word was limited to what I heard in chapel services, which I regularly attended, and at Sunday School.

One chief memory of Sunday School remains with me. I was asked, probably about the age of twelve, to read a paper to the class on the subject of Naaman. Whether the choice of theme was my own or the teacher's I cannot now say. But I well recollect that, just prior to the composition of the paper – 'composition' was an oft-used term in those days! – I had been much impressed by lines from a poem of Kipling:

> *Every secret self-revealing on the aching white-washed ceiling,*
> *Do you wonder that we draw ourselves from pain?*

Maybe I had come across them in the *British Weekly* which entered the home year in, year out. But my chief aim was, somehow or other, to weave these lines into my narrative, and I expect that I succeeded. But certain I am that the spiritual lessons of 2 Kings chapter 5 escaped my soul's notice.

I am puzzled by my parents' failure to give me a Bible of my own and to encourage me to read it, for in all educational matters, for instance, they were eager to see me make progress. They believed the Scriptures, but we did not read Scripture together in the home, nor did I know anything of family prayers, except on the infrequent occasions when we stayed overnight at the home of my mother's parents and when a large family Bible was opened and prayers raised. The religious exercises of my home were confined to the occasions when my father, sitting in the kitchen for warmth, would, in the hearing of the rest of the family, go through the notes of his sermons shortly before Sunday services. One such sermon, as I remember, was on the subject of Jephthah, but whether he held that Jephthah's daughter was sacrificed or not I cannot say. I certainly learned a little about Israel's famous judge in that way.

On one occasion, burned into my memory, I had committed a very serious fault, and it was only under very strong parental pressure that I had confessed to it. To this day, as it recurs to mind, I am still driven to find relief in the Psalmist's prayer: 'Remember not the sins of my youth, nor my transgressions: according to thy mercy remember thou me for thy goodness' sake, O Lord' (*Psalm 25:7*). My father's immediate relief, resulting from my confession of guilt, found expression in the gift of a book. I could wish that it had been a copy of the Word of God, but instead it was a Geography book: *The New Century Geographical Readers*, Book IVA: *The British*

Isles. Inscribed in it in his own fair hand are the words, 'To my boy Sidney, 4th February, 1909: The Lord bless thee . . . and keep thee'. There was no physical chastisement, but the event made a lifelong impression on my spirit, and after sixty-two years the tears of contrition are still inclined to flow as I think upon the occasion. It was such an occasion as might well lead to the reflection, 'there go I but for the grace of God'.

Looking back, as I now do, over half a century, I can see how different from the Methodism of the Wesleys' days was its twentieth-century development. Whether early Methodism was Calvinistic, as in the case of the Whitefield Methodists, or Arminian as linked with the two Wesleys, it was in both aspects Bible-loving and other-worldly. The blight of modernism lay still in the distant future. Doctrine, experience and practice were alike stressed. There was a spirituality, a cleaving to the living Lord, a whole-hearted belief in the full integrity of Scripture, a looking off from the things seen to things unseen, from the temporal to the spiritual, which characterised the first, second and third generations of Methodists. But by the time of my birth the fine gold had become dim. The gulf between the church and the world was closing fast. Radio, which completed the process and annealed the union, still lay some distance ahead; but the church into which I was born (so to speak) was already largely given over to 'modern thought' in its colleges and in its pulpits. Lord Tennyson, in his day, might sing of ringing in the true and ringing out the false, but the ringers of Methodism were 'ringing the changes' by abandoning the biblical doctrines to a large extent and welcoming doctrines 'which their fathers knew not'. Yet as a tyro I was convinced Wesleyan Methodism was Christian to a high degree, in fact all that could be desired of a Christian church.

[6]

Possibly my own personal case was typical of the changes that had been seen in the religious world. I was brought up to attend chapel, to think highly of Scripture (though my neglect of the reading of Scripture for myself might seem to be a more accurate reflex of the position), to regard the position of a minister as one of outstanding respectability and usefulness, and to view the church itself as an agency for spreading a God-appointed morality and the instrument for establishing the kingdom of God upon earth. But in the circle in which I moved, and which regarded the chapel as the chief centre of interest outside the home, the earlier insistence upon conversion and 'a closer walk with God' was rapidly giving place to an outlook of a very different kind. The separation from worldliness which had once been so clear-cut in Methodism was largely obliterated. Here and there survived a person who possessed something of the old evangelical fervour and the once-valued doctrine, but as year followed year they became rare indeed. I call to mind one such person. He was postmaster of the town in which I lived, and taught the Sunday School class to which I belonged. At the age of fourteen I found myself in hospital with acute appendicitis and among the letters I received was one from my teacher. Its content I have quite forgotten, but one item I can never forget. Pinned to the letter and written in red ink were the words, 'Is Christ precious to you?' My embarrassment was almost as acute as my bodily trouble. I wished to reply to the letter, but its inquiry troubled me greatly. Finally I answered the question affirmatively, but there was not true content in my words. I was still a stranger to grace and to God. But I chronicle the fact of the inquiry as evidence of the presence of a remnant of the truly godly in Methodist quarters.

As a youth – and I think that the experience that I now mention was completely typical of the era – I became enamoured of evolution. It had a strong appeal for me, and seemed to me to dovetail with the bare smattering of science that I had been taught. Precisely how it reached me I do not remember, but it was certainly strengthened by the books of a writer whose name is not by any means forgotten in these nineteen-seventies. I refer to Henry Drummond whose reputation in religious quarters was extremely high in my time of adolescence. He was by repute a Christian gentleman of the highest academic qualifications, active in evangelical circles – had he not played a considerable part in the Moody campaigns? – and one well able to show how the gospel of Christ could come to terms with evolution and the new scientific and philosophical ideas that were sweeping across the academic, not to say the ecclesiastical world with hurricane force. The strength and influence of Drummond's personality in his own day, particularly in student circles, were immense. Born in 1851, student of Divinity at New College, Edinburgh, devoted to his own particular brand of evangelism, he was appointed lecturer in Natural Science at the Free Church College, Glasgow, and later became a Professor of Theology. In academic circles he moved with the greatest ease. His addresses and writings won widespread attention. In 1883 appeared his *Natural Law in the Spiritual World*, a work which went through many editions. George Adam Smith, Drummond's biographer, assures his readers that 'the clear and simple style' of the book 'is charged with an enthusiasm, and carries a wealth of religious experience which captures the heart, and tempt [*sic*] the thoughtful reader to become indifferent to almost every prejudice which the introduction has excited in his mind'.

Drummond's book represents the attempt to bridge the gulf between the former belief in creation as based upon Scripture, and early Scripture in particular, and the teachings of Darwinism expounded first in *The Origin of*

[8]

Species (1859) and continued in such works as Darwin's *Descent of Man* (1871). The titles of Drummond's chapters indicate the general character of his book – biogenesis, degeneration, death, eternal life, environment, conformity to type, parasitism. It aimed at reconciling Darwinism and Christianity; but in working out his thesis Drummond virtually abandoned the old foundations of belief and framed a philosophy of the gospel which ill accords with 'the faith once delivered to the saints'.

Drummond's *Natural Law*, followed, in the order of my reading, by his *Tropical Africa* and his *Ascent of Man*, made an immense appeal to me, and gave me the idea that evolution was the key to spiritual problems, in fact the key to unlock the mysteries of religion. My scientific knowledge was scanty and superficial, but I had much interest in such phenomena as mimicry in nature and in all theories which set out to show that one species developed from another. *Tropical Africa* fanned the flame. I was certainly gullible. It would indeed almost be true to say that the gospel in which, at that time, I believed was evolution. As I write I cannot help but set down a line from John Newton's autobiographical poem: 'Alas, I knew not what I did'. Such was my enthusiasm that I virtually resolved to offer myself as a candidate for the Wesleyan ministry, and further, to offer myself as a missionary of the same Church to work in the Africa described by Drummond. It was as if an interest in grass-stalk insects and their power of shamming death, together with many other forms described in the book's chapter on mimicry, constituted a call to take the gospel to Africa. My missionary resolve was partly born of, and certainly stimulated by, a chapel service when I and two or three more teenagers were asked to give five-minute talks from the pulpit about aspects of the missionary enterprise. I need not say where my geographical choice fell. Not until conversion was my dream shattered.

For a period, then, I was a firm evolutionist. But at the same time, in the mercy of God, I held to the opinion that atonement through Christ must belong to my scheme. It became evident in the following way. Several of my older friends, youths of seventeen to twenty years of age, had adopted the practice of meeting together on Saturday evenings in one another's homes, and finally in one particular home, to discuss religious matters. I was most reluctant to join with them, but finally consented. It was their custom to produce and read 'papers' at their various sessions which formed the basis of discussion. One such paper was on the subject of the atonement, and I was rather shocked to discover that its author, the oldest member of the group, and its leader – he later became a Congregational minister, but died young – did not believe that the atonement of Calvary was an essential part of the Christian faith. His argument was that, in the Lord's Prayer, we ask for forgiveness 'as we forgive them that trespass against us'. But we demand no atonement from the one who has offended us: 'no more does God', said the leader. Despite my gross ignorance of Christian theology I sensed that the statement did not tally with the gospel, and I contrived to write some sort of reply, the first but by no means the last theological controversy in which I have been engaged. I am indeed reminded that, years later, after a series of brushes with others on matters biblical and theological, I felt that Jeremiah's lament had a measure of application to my own case: 'Woe is me, my mother, that thou hast borne me a man of strife and a man of contention to the whole earth!' (*Jer. 15:10*).

Actually when I wrote my reply (not without much copying from some of my father's books), my ignorance was abysmal. My general notion of religious truth was that, as spontaneous generation was an impossibility, – I had learned that from Drummond – there must be some 'divine spark' within man which could be fanned into a flame, to become the nucleus of a Christian life. In other words I had the notion that 'eternal life' was implanted within man from birth, and that, furthermore, works (I use the term theologically) constituted the way to God and heaven. I was impressed by the words which, somewhere and somehow, I had picked up:

> *To do my best and let that stand*
> *The record of my brain and hand;*
> *This, I believe, is all I need*
> *For my philosophy and creed.*

Clearly I had no knowledge of my need of divine help and of the gospel of Christ. At that time 'works' was my gospel. I was naturally religious, as a friend or onlooker told me later. But of the Lord and his saving work, of Scripture and its vital message, I obviously knew nothing, indeed less than nothing. All was vanity.

But such ignorance proved no hindrance to my entering upon a career as a Methodist preacher. Wesleyanism was greatly attached to the 'local preacher' system, and the work of 'local preaching' belonged to both sides of the family. One grandparent and my own father held, or were later to hold, illuminated certificates congratulating them upon three score or more years of service in this very capacity; an uncle had entered the Wesleyan ministry; another, refused by a Methodist synod and college, had been accepted in the Anglican ministry; several uncles were local preachers. I succumbed to the pressure. My father had little difficulty in persuading the Superintendent minister of the circuit to 'put me on the plan', not on 'full plan' at first, but on probation. I was seventeen years of age at the time.

Here again, strange as it may sound, my first text reached to the very centre of the Christian faith. But my sermon could not have been based upon the text, for I was still ignorant of the first rudiments of that faith. My choice fell upon 1 Corinthians 2:2: 'I determined not to know any thing among you, save Jesus Christ, and him crucified'. My knowledge of the Lord and his cross was of the most superficial kind, not worthy of being termed knowledge. I gathered together a few sentences from various authors, including, as I still remember, the words that Pharaoh was a midge and Caesar a midget in comparison with the writer of this First Epistle to the Corinthians; but of Christ crucified I knew not a thing beyond the bare historical record. Apparently, however, the 'full local' who accompanied me on the occasion reported favourably on my efforts, for I was shortly placed on 'full plan', or else – for I forget the exact detail at this point – I was about to be so placed, when both on my own side and on that of the Superintendent minister, this course became undesirable. In other words, my conversion intervened, and with my conversion, by the grace of God other forces came into operation which drew me, ere long, into religious company of a very different type, and changed the entire course of my life.

2: *The Early End of a Ministerial Career in Methodism*

For almost the whole of 1918, the last year of the First
World War, I served of necessity in the Armed Forces, the
first half of the year in England, the second half in the
Somme region of France. To my very considerable relief
of mind, not to say of body, after two or three weeks spent
in a French base camp, preparatory to being sent up to the
actual war front in the days when Sir Douglas Haig had
reported that 'we had our backs to the wall', I was given a
medical check-up and rated as below par for front-line
action, though personally I was unaware that anything
ailed me. I had been awarded a 'stripe' for efficiency on the
parade ground, and had received the usual small increase
in pay as being a first-class shot. At this point of time I was
relegated to a quiet country château where the sounds and
sights of war rarely disturbed the peace. It was the
headquarters of a Searchlight Unit (Royal Engineers) and
for the first and last time in my life I found myself an
engineer. But my duties were administrative and clerical,
not at all practical. I remained in seclusion until the end of
the year, when again, to my great relief (for I might have
been detained in military service for a long period after the
Armistice of November 11, 1918), I was demobilised
speedily, the result of my membership of the local
government service in civil life. I left France on New
Year's Day, 1919, and ended my military career on the
exact day of the month that had seen its commencement.

In regard to Christian matters the year in the Forces was a time of severe testing, but I believe that, by the grace of God, there was a measure of spiritual growth, though not in great depth, and an increased knowledge of the Lord and his ways. While stationed in the homeland I maintained contact, as far as possible, with Methodist circles, and in the providence of God I was brought into contact also with men who bore a faithful witness to Christ. One occasion I particularly remember. In the training camp men were housed in huts, about thirty per hut. It was by no means pleasant for one like myself, who had been brought up, by comparison, in a religious atmosphere, to be in such close proximity to men who drank and swore and exchanged coarse jokes without compunction. But it happened that, one day, I was transferred from one hut to another, and in the late hours found myself located alongside a man who had the courage to kneel down to pray before getting to rest. To me he was a Godsend. He introduced me to several others of similar convictions, and in so doing strengthened my own poor and feeble witness to 'the way of life'.

At the same time prayer became to me a more real experience and exercise, a more rewarding activity. I received what I learned to regard as providential answers to my petitions. One such answer impressed me much. It occurred some four months after my 'call up', by which time I was thoroughly homesick, for I had never been absent from home before, except for the usual brief holiday week of the year's summer. The 'short leave' early promised by the commanding officer was put off time after time, but delay only stimulated my prayers. At length a day arrived when I felt an inward persuasion that I would get home during the ensuing few days. My longing was granted, but in totally unexpected fashion, not through the normal channels. The weather had been severe, winds on the parade ground had been cold and keen. A recruit had died. His body was returned to his home town for burial. A military 'firing party' was required to be at the grave-side. The battalion contained several hundred men – well over a thousand, I imagine – and of these some six or eight were required. I was one of the chosen few. Furthermore, the place of burial was only about eight miles distant from my home. We made the journey and were to be lodged in a public house. Would the officer in charge allow me leave of absence overnight? Would he be fearful lest I should not return in time for the grave-side ceremony? He refused such leave to others, he gave it to me. I learned that God can bring about answers to prayers in most unexpected ways. I learned that he can take factors belonging to a variety of situations and dovetail them together in a way that causes the suppliant to say, 'It is the Lord's doing and marvellous in our eyes'.

My new Christian companions strengthened my growing convictions that the Scripture lay at the very centre of the Christian faith and life. A chaplain of the army, conducting a voluntary class for men in training, suggested that we should study a newly-published book entitled *As Tommy Sees Us* (that is, Thomas Atkins). My companions endeavoured to turn his mind in a different direction, arguing that their souls needed the Word itself rather than a book which was but ephemeral. Their plea carried the day. My own convictions derived fresh strength. My experiences overseas caused me to feel a need of Christ as never before. As yet I knew little of him; my soul was thirsty. I came to know that true religion could neither begin with myself nor terminate with myself. I saw the hand of God also in diverting me from the trench warfare in which I had expected to have to participate. I entertained a stronger dislike than hitherto for 'the spirit of the world'. But as yet, through lack of long and serious application, my knowledge of the Word remained small. In France there was nothing of Christian fellowship at hand, though once a week I tramped some five or six miles from the château into the nearest town where a chaplain conducted a well-attended Forces service. His name was Tiplady. I remember nothing of the addresses he gave, but I have little reason to suppose that his doctrine corresponded with that of the Toplady of eighteenth-century fame. Had it done so I think that I should have been given a stronger impression of 'the truth as it is in Jesus'. But the chaplain's task was certainly a difficult one.

Not long after my return home a completely new factor entered my life. Seven years later it resulted in marriage. In other words the Lord led me to the one who ultimately became 'the wife of my youth' and an untold blessing to me, as also did her parents. My introduction to her parents and her home meant for me that life had acquired a completely new dimension. So far my knowledge of Christian homes was confined to those of Methodist persuasion. I have previously said that, in my own home, chapel affairs were central, and this was the case with the home of my new friends, but in the first case the centrality was little more than social; it hardly possessed a spiritual quality, whereas the new home to which the Lord now gave me access possessed a godliness and a spiritual quality of a marked and refreshing kind. For here was a home in which the Bible was central; family prayer was observed with regularity; chapel attendance betokened a quest for increased knowledge of the Lord and of his salvation. Here was spiritual reality; doctrine mattered profoundly; the world, with its pernicious ways and misleading concepts, was to be put out of doors. The church was regarded, not as a social centre, where Saturday night jollifications could take place, and where billiards and badminton might well occupy other week-evenings, but as the church of the living God, owning allegiance to the will of God as made known in the Scriptures. I was profoundly impressed.

My quest was not at all easy, though I was reminded by an outsider that faint heart never won fair lady. After all, I was very much of an outsider, known only as a very distant school acquaintance. But the Lord came to my aid. My future mother-in-law (Mrs B. M. Yarwood) was strongly and inwardly moved to regard me favourably, even when her knowledge of me was very slight. I can only come to the conclusion that it was the Lord who laid me as a burden upon her heart. She learned that I was religiously inclined, for I early let the family know that entry upon the Wesleyan Methodist ministry was my aim and ambition, and it became her ambition, as it were, no less than that of her husband, to 'teach me the law of the Lord more perfectly'. In fact they became to me as Aquila and Priscilla. So my visits to their home were times of fervent discussion on the things of God; invariably so except for one occasion when, for a reason I failed to understand, conversation remained on a lower plane. This new phase in my life came during the days when, after my military career ended, I had resumed service as a 'local preacher' with the Wesleyan body. I must explain that my new friends were members of a Strict and Particular Baptist Church, that is to say, strict in respect of admission to the Lord's table, particular in that they held to particular redemption, that is, to an atonement which had respect only to the elect of God. For the first time I came into contact, and I must add, into conflict with Calvinistic doctrine.

A happening that belonged to the life of Mrs Yarwood will serve to illustrate the experimental aspect of her and her husband's Christianity. It opened my eyes to a type of

experience to which hitherto I had been a complete
stranger. Some twelve years previous to my acquaintance
with her she had felt strongly moved by the Holy Spirit
to enter into church fellowship, and this involved an
appearance before church members to 'give her testimony' to salvation and divine leadings, followed, if
accepted, by baptism by immersion. But she felt a secret
dread lest, when she appeared before the church, she
might find herself speechless, and she applied herself
earnestly to the Lord on the matter. Faith, we are
assured, obtains promises (*Heb. 11:33*), and the Lord
answered her request by impressing a word from Luke
8:48 powerfully upon her heart: 'Daughter, be of good
comfort: thy faith hath made thee whole; go in peace'.
But then, with increasing boldness, she asked the Lord
to confirm his word of promise by causing the minister at
the next Lord's Day service to take Luke 8:48 as his text.
Her exercise of soul would be quite unknown to him for
he was a visiting preacher. Mr Yarwood later described
the case to me as one where his wife, like Gideon, wanted
her fleece both wet and dry in turn. The day of worship
duly arrived, the preacher announced his text, and it was
not that for which the suppliant had prayed. But it soon
became evident that the preacher was not happy with his
choice of text. His words were few and stumbling, and
shortly he came to a complete halt. 'Friends', he said, 'I
find that I cannot speak from this passage, and must take
another text'. The rest of his discourse was based upon
the words so eagerly awaited by the suppliant in the pew.
In due time her testimony was given to the church,
baptism followed, and much happiness resulted. Exercise of soul is certainly one mark of the Christian
pathway. In later years her testimony, spoken to her
husband, ran thus: 'I could not live if the Lord did not
hear and answer my prayers'.

The writer pauses in his narrative to add that, many years later, he found a passage in one of Spurgeon's sermons which furnishes an expert comment on the ministerial dilemma just mentioned. It is as follows: 'How singularly at times you have heard your case described! You have gone to the house of God, and sat down in the pew, and the minister has gone into the pulpit and taken a text just adapted to yourself; he begins to tell you what your position is exactly; and then he tells you the way you should go. You cannot help saying as you retire, "That man is a prophet". Ay, and so he is. I have often told you this is the way to be a servant of the Lord. Daniel was acknowledged to be a true servant of the Lord because he could tell the king both the dream and its interpretation. The astrologers could only tell the interpretation after they had been told the dream. Many can give you advice when they know your case. But the true servant of the Lord does not want to be informed about your case; he knows it beforehand. You come up here, unobserved by your fellow-creatures; but what you have done in your home, that the Lord has told His servant . . . it has been revealed to him in secret communion, and it will be made manifest to your conscience'.

To resume: up to this point in time my theology had been thin and poor. It lacked substance as much as it lacked virility. It was certainly not theology in depth. I had given it surprisingly little attention, and its development had suffered from my ignorance of the Word. But now began a new chapter in my life. I gave greatly increased attention to the Testaments both Old and New. As Calvinistic doctrine for the first time reached my ears and alarmed my soul, it became my first ambition to defend the Arminianism of Wesleyan Methodism. After each visit to what after a time virtually became my home from home, I returned to utilise the parental bookshelves to bolster up my arguments. I had to learn a new vocabulary. Such terms as election, predestination, justification, sanctification, and their like, though not completely unknown to me before, assumed a new significance. The term 'free will' in particular came to the forefront. Previously I had hardly considered its content; I had assumed that the freedom of the human will was incapable of contradiction. Now, too, for the first time in my life, I was compelled by dire necessity to explore the Scriptures. It affected my preaching. It could not help but do so. I became more doctrinal. My Arminianism tended to wane. The 'force of truth' (to adopt the famous phrase which meant so much to Thomas Scott) drove me into corners. Usually, during my repeated visits to my home from home, I took a slip of paper on which I had written my 'Arminian texts', mostly culled from the sermons of John Wesley himself. I did so on a date which I have forgotten – it was probably in the early summer, 1919 – and ere I left after heartfelt discussions I had surrendered the slip to the flames; which is to say that I had become convinced of the scripturalness of Calvinistic doctrine. Of course, in later days and years I found it necessary to go much more deeply into all aspects of that doctrine, but for the moment I was satisfied. Many problems, as I realised, lay ahead, but in a new way I had found Scripture a satisfying portion. The inspiration and the integrity of the Word now appeared to me in a new light.

The further effect upon my preaching can readily be imagined. I had been especially impressed by the Pauline teaching in 1 Corinthians chapter 2 that 'the natural man receiveth not the things of the Spirit of God: for they are foolishness unto him: neither can he know them, because they are spiritually discerned' (v.14). In fact I now composed a sermon on that text as also upon Acts 4:12: 'Neither is there salvation in any other; for there is none other name under heaven given among men, whereby we must be saved'. The latter was the last text I used in a Wesleyan pulpit at that time. My congregations reacted unfavourably, and ere long my career as a 'local preacher' reached its close.

Meanwhile a new linked factor had entered my life. After much inward conflict I had begun to pay occasional visits to the chapel where my new friends worshipped. Though but a mile from my home I had never heard of it previously. It soon became my Bethel. Again I was deeply impressed. One thing which struck me forcibly was the lack in this particular instance – though probably not common in the denomination – of a 'professional ministry'. The minister followed a strenuous business career – he had been a coal controller during the World War – but simultaneously he fulfilled his pastoral commitments. Then, too, he did not use 'notes' in preaching; I learned that they were frowned upon, and indeed quite disallowed, by the denomination. But above all I was impressed by the solemnity of divine things, with the freedom from worldly custom, and with the firm faith of the worshippers in the full dependability of the Word of God. Modernism was conspicuously absent from thought as well as practice. The apostolic warning against yielding to 'every wind of doctrine' seemed totally unnecessary in this case, for the same wind blew month in month out from the one quarter – Geneva – except that the baptism of believers by immersion was followed, while infant baptism was sternly condemned.

My Methodist parents were very much alarmed, not to say distressed, by the new developments, and especially so when they learned that, occasionally, I was attending a service at a non-Methodist chapel. They still clung to the hope that I might one day be an ordained Methodist minister. But my convictions were sufficiently strong to surmount their remonstrances. One occasion I recall with particular clarity. It happened that 'Aquila and Priscilla' and their family were in a distant place on holiday; nevertheless I felt a powerful constraint to attend their chapel in their absence. Accordingly I found myself at the evening service. When sermon time arrived the minister explained that during the afternoon of the day he had himself been under strong constraint to lay aside the text of his earlier choice and instead to preach upon another, namely, Acts 22:16: 'And now why tarriest thou? arise, and be baptised, and wash away thy sins, calling on the name of the Lord'. I retained little of the sermon's content; it was the text that gripped my soul like the grip of a vice; not the whole of it, but in particular its opening question, 'Why tarriest thou?' It came to me as a clarion call to sever my links with Methodism and to cast in my lot with a people whose outlook on many matters differed profoundly from that of those with whom I had been reared. It was some months later, however, before I took the step of applying for baptism. Ultimately I did so, being convinced that the New Testament warranted the baptism of none but believers. Thus it was that my parents' hope of ministerial appointment for their son was frustrated. The tension was for a time severe on both sides, but the healing virtues of time and the mercies of God later restored good relations, and doubtless they observed that my acceptance of Calvinistic doctrine had no adverse effect on character: I trust the exact reverse was the case.

Some little time after my introduction to those whom I might almost dare to call my 'godparents', I was presented with two small books. One was Gadsby's Hymn-book, which enjoyed a monopoly in the Strict and Particular Baptist Churches, also called Gospel Standard Churches after the denominational magazine which circulated among them. It was edited at that time by J. K. Popham of Brighton, to whose occasional ministry in the Lancashire area my fiancée (as she shortly became) owed much initial spiritual blessing. This hymn-book, I learned and noted, had been a potent factor in holding the denomination to its Calvinistic creed. The other book I must mention at slightly greater length. Its title was *Out of the Depths*, an editor's title, presumably derived from Psalm 130:1, and applied to a reprint of John Newton's autobiography. It had been read by the donor at a time when she knew me to be in France surrounded by sundry perils, and from it she learned that Newton, in his days of profligacy, had been preserved, in a sense, from worse things than actually befell him, by his love for a certain Mary Catlett whom afterwards he married. If I remember the case aright, she was a mere thirteen years of age when he first went to sea. In her mind my friend visualized me in similar peril, prayed for me, befriended me on my return to the homeland, and presented me with the Newton book. On its flyleaf were inscribed her words of benediction:

> To Sidney, given with much prayer, hoping and believing that the same grace that brought John Newton 'out of the depths' has brought him; from his affectionate friend, B. M. Yarwood.

The date was May 5, 1919. Little wonder, therefore, that Newton's career and writings attracted my strong interest, and that I gave them a degree of attention greater than that accorded to many other of the long procession of witnesses. In later years I was able to visit Olney (Bucks.) and to see there, still preserved in the upper room of the vicarage, the board on which 'the African blasphemer' (as Newton ever reminded himself) had had two texts painted, and positioned over the mantelpiece, to keep him in mind of the grace that had followed him and would not

let him go: 'Since thou wast precious in my sight, thou
hast been honourable', but 'Thou shalt remember that
thou wast a bondman in the land of Egypt, and the Lord
thy God redeemed thee' (*Isa. 43:4, Deut. 15:15*).

Later I was able to acquire a one-volume edition of the
whole of Newton's writings, including his contributions
to the Olney Hymns, his letters (a selection has gone
through several editions under the title of *Cardiphonia*),
and his sermons. The sermons, though useful, possess no
especial merit, but the letters are priceless. Those entitled
'To a Wife', covering the period 1750 to 1785, include
much material of biographical interest. I have long felt
that any Christian who has not made acquaintance with
Newton and his works tends to lack a spiritual dimension.
It was a joy to me in later years to find, in a second-hand
bookshop in Norwich, a copy of Newton's *Review of
Ecclesiastical History during the First Century*, bearing the
date 1770. It carried an inscription in the author's own
hand stating, 'To my very dear friend Mr James Armit-
age, from the Author'. It now forms part of a collection of
books and documents which I esteem as among permissible earthly treasures. The collection contains letters of
Isaac Watts, James Montgomery (hymn writer), C. H.
Spurgeon, J. C. Ryle, and men of lesser fame; also the
signatures of such worthies as Charles Simeon, Philip
Doddridge, George Müller, John Angell James, the Earl
of Shaftesbury, S. P. Tregelles, Handley Moule, Hugh
Stowell (hymn writer) and others. From time to time I
inspect them with deep regard. The signatures I have
acquired by tearing out the flyleaves of presentation copies
of the various works in which they appeared.

3: *New Circles and Old Books*

It is hardly necessary for me to say that my Calvinistic doctrine was anathema to my parents and my near relations who were Methodists to a man. The doctrine that seemed most of all to meet with their disapproval was that of particular redemption. My mother remarked to me one day: 'He is a silly, foolish God who would send his Son into the world to die for a part of mankind only, and not die to redeem everyone'; my uncle who was a Methodist minister of over thirty years' standing termed the doctrine blasphemy. Simultaneously I lost the friendship of one who, while belonging to my own district, had also been my valued companion during a portion of my days in the Forces. He, like myself, had reached the conclusion that he ought to offer himself for the Methodist ministry. Looking back after long years, I seem to remember that he belonged to the United Methodist Church, for the reunion of the three chief Methodist Churches still lay a dozen or more years ahead. It was after demobilisation that our friendship came to grief. I wrote to him one day, after the events described in the previous chapter, and of course after my own ministerial ambitions had vanished into thin air, and in reference to his own similar ambition I commented: 'Do not become a minister if you can help it'. Immediately the fat was in the fire. I intended the words in the same sense as I discovered years later in the writings of Spurgeon; in other words I intended to warn my friend that only an overpowering and irresistible conviction that entry into the ministry was God's will for him could justify his giving up other employment and going forward. But he interpreted the message in a very different sense, and almost immediately our friendship came to an abrupt end. Fifty years later I discovered his name in an official list of Methodist ministers, and I wrote to him reminding him of our old and close friendship, telling him a little of my own experiences in the intervening years, and enquiring about his own sentiments after so long a time. Whether or not my letter reached him I do not know, for I received no reply. As is the case with many Christians I had to learn that the truth of God can divide man from man, as it can also unite hearts and souls in unbreakable bonds.

I entered upon membership of the Strict and Particular Baptist Church as one who had very much to learn of the things and ways of the Lord. But I was helped to give heed to those ways, and I trust that from the human standpoint, both my own and that of onlookers and fellow-Christians, I made progress in the divine life. I knew that I was no longer what I had been previously. J. K. Popham, whom I have already mentioned, in a sermon which I heard him deliver, or it may have been in an article contributed to the magazine he edited, had quoted a saying of Martin Luther that 'doctrine is heaven'; and I began to find a glimmer of that truth in my own soul. I was introduced to books which were as green pastures in which I was free to feed, to preaching which differed fundamentally from all that I had previously heard, to fellowship in the things of God which was more genuinely like 'the real thing' than aught that I had earlier known.

I benefited, too, from the occasional ministry of men other than Baptists. Among them was the Rev Henry Atherton, minister of Grove Chapel, Camberwell, London, who always signed himself 'Henry Atherton: Eph. 2.8'. He had been brought up as a Wigan miner, probably the son of a miner, and his speech and personality certainly gave one the impression that he had been brought 'out of the depths'. Occasionally he visited South Lancashire on behalf of the Sovereign Grace Union of which he had become reviver and General Secretary. He was a personification of vigour and resolution. He presented me with two or three books and in a later year (1925) persuaded me to contribute a paper on justification to the Annual Meeting of the Union held in Camberwell. It is printed in abridged form in the Annual Report of that year. On one occasion, probably in 1923, when I happened to be in London, he persuaded me to accompany him, together with Basil Brunning, a friendly minister and also the Union's Organising Secretary, to the spot in the City known as the Angel where an S.G.U. meeting had been arranged. He attended, if I remember aright, in an ordinary workman's cap to show himself a member of the working classes, one whom the 'common people' might hear gladly. At the meeting I recollect saying a few halting, stammering words: I was new to public speaking. Beginners need all the sympathy we can invoke.

Another S.G.U. speaker in my home area (the Manchester district) was the Rev Frederick Peacock whose manner of speech was such that he readily called to mind the Lord's word to Job: 'Gavest thou the goodly wings unto the peacocks?' (39:13). He was an Anglican minister settled in a so-called Chapel of Ease at Buxton. Some of his hearers were inclined to describe the duration of his address as a time of 'heaven upon earth'. His beaming fresh countenance gave added force to his utterance, especially when he held forth – an occasion long held in the memory – on the theme, 'Yea, he is altogether lovely'. He had delineated the 'beauty of the Lord' in the earlier words of the Song, and as he reached the climax of blessing, some who listened afterwards reported that they had all but entered the third heaven. They considered that he had almost shown them 'the King in his beauty, without a veil between'.

Henry Atherton encouraged me in another direction. He arranged for the S.G.U. to print an address I had prepared on 'The Life and Times of William Tyndale'. It appeared in pamphlet form in 1927. Actually it was an address delivered at an auxiliary of the Trinitarian Bible Society two or three years earlier. My interest in the martyr, already considerable, was thereby much augmented: it long remained an incentive to 'abound in the work of the Lord', for, after all, all present-day believers whose native tongue is English owe to the great translator of Scripture an incalculable debt. In his best-known portrait, Tyndale's index finger is shown pointing to the Holy Scriptures, while, in Latin, we are told:

> *That light o'er all thy darkness, Rome,*
> *In triumph might arise,*
> *An exile freely I become,*
> *Freely a sacrifice.*

A reminder that sacrifice for the Lord's sake, even unto death, well becomes the children of God!

The ministry of the Baptist church to which I now belonged furnished me with much food for thought. Membership was by no means large, but there was growth, and in the early 'twenties it was judged that the time had come for rebuilding the premises on the same site. The new building was opened in 1925, but by that time my residence in the area was about to end, as my profession took me elsewhere. I regret to have to add that the church fell later upon somewhat sad days, and finally, as its membership became so enfeebled that it was unable to continue to hold services – they had long been of the 'read sermon' variety – it was judged best by the surviving trustees to sell the property and, I presume, to devote the proceeds to denominational purposes.

My active membership dated from 1920 to 1925. I had not long been a member before I found myself perplexed by a matter which I set myself to investigate. It really resolved itself into the question of Calvinism as opposed to and distinct from Hyper-Calvinism. In the first instance the element of mystery was occasioned by the fact that I shortly began to notice a marked difference between the preaching of Strict and Particular Baptist ministers and the language and teaching of certain of the books and authors which were recommended as worthy of the attention of church members, and indeed of all Christians. I refer here to books of the past, those of Puritans and others. Bunyan, for example, was highly commended, not only because he happened to be a Baptist, but as an outstanding case of all that a Christian minister ought to be in the pulpit, in the home and in the world, and as a writer of the utmost reliability. Thus far I had little knowledge of Bunyan, although I had some slight acquaintance with his *Pilgrim's Progress* in both its parts. As I read more widely in his writings I perceived that there was a freeness and openness about his invitations and exhortations to saints and sinners alike which found no counterpart in the preaching from the Baptist pulpits known to me. I was to learn later that there were several kinds of Strict Baptists. The type to which my words specially refer was that known as 'the Gospel Standard', some even being prepared to speak of 'the Gospel Standard denomination of Strict and Particular Baptists'. The Gospel Standard ministers (and I discovered that there was a jealously guarded and much scrutinised list of such men), I found, did not believe it right to exhort unbelievers to repent and believe the gospel, and their exhortations to believers, I learned, were also oblique and rarely, if ever, direct, except as they conveyed them in the very language of Scripture. Thus they would not say 'Draw near to God', but 'May the Lord help us to draw near to Him'; not 'Do what the Lord tells you to do', but 'May the Lord help us so to do'. They seemed to be fearful of putting the responsibility for obedience upon either believer or unbeliever.

In the case of the unbeliever, their line of thought forbade it, for in fact they had 'hold of the wrong end of the stick'. Their argument ran thus:

First: The unbeliever is dead in trespasses and sins.

Second: A dead man (and therefore the unbeliever) is incapable of hearing a command from another, from a minister, and is clearly quite unable to render obedience to a command.

Third: It cannot therefore be right for a minister to bid a man do what, as a dead man, he is wholly unable to do.

Fourth: Such a command would involve the minister in the root error of free will.

Hence they confined their message, as far as the unbeliever was concerned, to warning him of the consequences of sin and of continuance in sin, without exhorting him to turn from his sin and embrace the saving message of the gospel. The minister to whom I listened regularly told me firmly and frankly that on no account whatsoever was he prepared to tell a sinner to repent and believe the gospel.

Not so Bunyan and other Puritans and men of mark in the long history of the Christian church! George Whitefield, for instance, was admired as a Calvinist, and his stand against the Arminian doctrine of the Wesleys was applauded; but not a few, when brought face to face with the eloquence of Whitefield's exhortations to all and sundry, were prepared to hold up their hands in horror and to say 'Free will, Free will!' If it was pointed out to them that the Lord himself began his ministry with the words, spoken to men at large, 'Repent ye, and believe the gospel', they thrust the thought from them, as it were, spoke of the twentieth century being different from the first, and left the matter unresolved.

Strangely enough, hymns were to be found in *Gadsby* which illustrated the very form of words which the pulpit condemned, or at least which it refused to employ. Thus in the noble hymn of Joseph Hart dealing with the theme of the brazen serpent and its gospel application, ('When the chosen tribes debated, 'gainst their God, as hardly treated', No. 876) – an excellent exposition both in style and language – the dying sinner, after being informed of his malady and of ways in which it is impossible to find healing, is instructed that Christ crucified is God's way of salvation, whereupon he is exhorted to 'Look and live!' It would be fatuous to argue that Hart is not addressing a dead sinner but a dying sinner, for this would involve a denial of the doctrine of 'total depravity'. Hart's exhortation occurs in the last line of his hymn. And it was this particular point that was burked by the Gospel Standard pulpit, though the evidence that it was fully warranted by Scripture was to be found in many old writings held in the greatest respect and frequently quoted (as far as 'safety' allowed) in the denominational magazine.

The minister to whom I have referred was not harsh and completely unsympathetic to what I said, though he put it from him. He had given me an unusual but serviceable baptismal text on the occasion of my 'burial with Christ by baptism into death'. It was taken from 1 Kings 20:11: 'Let not him that girdeth on his harness boast himself as he that putteth it off'; but I could not but note his stern resolution never to bid a sinner repent of his sins or indeed to do anything at all. My perplexity continued. And yet slowly I was beginning to perceive what I took to be the root cause of the difficulty, or at least a historical landmark pointing to the root cause. I must refer at this point to Articles of Faith. The church of my membership possessed Articles of its own, those to which I had subscribed at the time of my baptism. They were not identical with those known as the Gospel Standard Articles, but belonged, I believe, to an earlier period of church history and may even have been as old as the period ending with the death of Dr John Gill in 1771. I had reason to think so, for on investigation I found a phraseology in them which was very similar to, if not completely identical with, a Confession of Faith approved and probably drawn up by Dr Gill.

I next learned to my sorrow that in or about the year 1878 Articles formerly approved in Gospel Standard circles, after considerable disputing, had been supplemented by four Added Articles. On account of their importance in the eyes of the friends among whom I moved I quote three of them:

Art. XXXII: We believe that it would be unsafe, from the brief records we have of the way in which the apostles, under the immediate direction of the Lord, addressed their hearers in certain special cases and circumstances, to derive absolute and universal rules for ministerial addresses in the present day under widely-different circumstances. And we further believe that an assumption that others have been inspired as the apostles were has led to the grossest errors amongst both Romanists and professed Protestants.

Art. XXXIII: Therefore, for ministers in the present day to address unconverted persons, or indiscriminately all in a mixed congregation, calling upon them to savingly repent, believe, and receive Christ, or perform any other acts dependent upon the new creative power of the Holy Ghost, is, on the one hand, to imply creature power, and on the other, to deny the doctrine of special redemption.

Art. XXXIV: We believe that any such expressions as convey to the hearers the belief that they possess a certain power to flee to the Saviour, to close in with Christ, to receive Christ, while in an unregenerate state, so that unless they do thus close with Christ, etc., they shall perish, are untrue, and must, therefore, be rejected. And we further believe that we have no Scripture warrant to take the exhortations in the Old Testament intended for the Jews in national covenant with God, and apply them in a spiritual and saving sense to unregenerated man.

For me the matter was not confined to the theological realm alone; it had its practical side, for an element in the church which had received me into fellowship considered that it would be wise for the Articles of Faith already in use to be discarded in favour of the Gospel Standard Articles, including the added ones; a moderately strong current ran in that direction. It was doubtless supposed that it would place the church fairly and squarely within the Gospel Standard circle of churches, and that it might yield to the local church and possibly to certain of its individual members additional benefits. But as I and several others, including my particular friends, thought on the matter, the more we became convinced that we must contend for the retention of the older set of Articles. We felt that the Added Articles virtually stated that it is unsafe to follow the Scriptures in respect of the ministry of the gospel. They 'put it across' that the brevity of the reports of apostolic sermons, linked with the circumstantial differences between ancient and modern times, rendered it unsafe for the latter-day preacher to use the sermons as valid specimens of gospel preaching fitted to the need of Victorian or later times. This virtually amounted to a repudiation of the all-sufficiency of Scripture in the most vital of problems and procedures. It certainly conflicted with the methods and procedures of Puritans and others whose basic Calvinistic doctrines and principles none could well call into question. What it amounted to was the claim that preaching in the modern age must be attuned to the principles of a Hyper-Calvinistic theology. In addressing unsaved sinners preachers must not follow apostolic precedent.

As my knowledge of the matter increased, so did my concern that my church membership should not involve me in the acceptance of such an alarming error. At the same time it gave me an understanding of the obvious reluctance of certain preachers to preach as did the apostles. The problem caused a certain amount of dissension in the church of my allegiance. It had an important side-issue also, namely, an almost one-hundred-per-cent lack of interest in missionary endeavour. Indeed, I learned to my consternation that 'missionary work' was all but placed under the ban as being one aspect of Arminianism. If one here or there showed some interest in the evangelisation of the heathen, he was given to understand that the cause of God in the homeland should monopolise his wandering attention. The tragedy was that such a view was sincerely and genuinely held. It was several years before I learned that there were other branches of the Strict Baptist denomination which did not hold these restricted and perverted views.

Furthermore, with certain church members there was a somewhat strange outlook on the ministerial office. It was agreed by all that any church member who claimed to have received a divine call to minister the Word must seek and obtain church approval and commendation before engaging in the work, and offering his services to other churches within the denomination; it was tacitly assumed that there would be no question of his services being offered outside the denomination. But a leading figure was once heard to express the view – and I had reason to think that it was most tenaciously held – 'I will see to it that no one goes out from this church'. He meant, of course, a going out for ministry. His view was that the ministerial office was so exalted as to be all but unattainable except, perchance, to the rarest of mortals. The same person held that it was inadvisable to give support to such organisations as the Sovereign Grace Union for they introduced church members to ministry which might at some points be in conflict with that officially and denominationally approved. Happily such a 'tight' view was held by comparatively few.

I noted as years went by that a further tendency of the ministry, which I could not but deplore, was to raise such barriers to church membership as hindered those who year after year 'sat under the ministry' but who never 'made a profession' of salvation. As I write I think of the cases of men whom I knew, and knew well, of whose salvation there was little doubt. But the ministry was of such a character that they were left to continue in a profession-less state without any urge from without to declare themselves and join themselves to the church of God. I think of cases where this continued until the individuals were seventy, eighty, or even ninety years of age; they occupied their seats in the house of the Lord, but like a door on its hinges they made no progress towards 'union with Zion'. Their private lives, walk and conversation, supplied good evidence of the Spirit's work in their hearts, but they died as they lived – outside the visible church of God. They were lifelong worshippers with the congregation, but never submitted themselves to baptism, never attended the Lord's table, never assisted the saints of the Lord by engaging in audible prayer in meetings for prayer.

[35]

These things being said, I hasten to add that both among ministers and people I knew some who were the deeply-exercised disciples of the Lord and who honoured their profession of his name by their humble, godly, prayerful mode of living. As I made acquaintance with them both inside and outside my immediate local circle, I learned much from them and their ways, and knew them to be among 'the salt of the earth'. Their hospitality was gracious, their 'works' altruistic, their 'patience of hope' remarkable. In them was 'fulfilled all the good pleasure of God's goodness, and the work of faith with power'. It befell that for a period in the earlier nineteen-twenties I needed to live and work in London for some eight to twelve weeks or more. Two families extended to me their weekend hospitality, enabling me to attend upon the ministry of Mr George Rose of Croydon (formerly of Cranbrook, Kent). At the age of about ninety he ended his pilgrimage a few years ago, but not before bequeathing to posterity a record of his providential pathway and spiritual experiences in a book entitled *Remembered Mercies Recorded*. It was published in 1952. His wife and a close friend of hers wrote me a number of truly spiritual letters after I returned home, and I still keep them among my Christian 'treasures'.

As time went on, my desire to become better acquainted with Christian literature of worth grew rapidly. My conversion had resulted in the shedding of the literature of my Arminian days, and I began to gather, as opportunity offered, the writings of men whose praise was in the mouth of every knowledgeable Calvinist. I had inherited from my father a measure of his bookish interests, and this facilitated my quest. But study is assisted by opportunity for giving out as well as of taking in; hence the wise advice once given to a vacation student by an 'old hand': 'If you wish to learn get a teaching post'. In my case the minister and deacons of the church decided to put me in charge of a Sunday School class. I soon found the exercise very profitable to myself. My first assignment – it may have been my own choice, I forget – was the Epistle to the Hebrews. Ignorant as I still was of the variety of available commentaries on that Epistle I turned to the voluminous work of John Owen (I had been given his twenty-four volumes by a Christian friend in the legal profession whose leisure did not suffice for the reading of them), spending time at the outset on his two preliminary volumes of 'Exercitations', and proceeding to dip into the detailed comments of the succeeding six volumes, even though my charges were but young teenagers. The exercise proved as valuable to me as I trust it did for them. It was my introduction to the wealth of exposition of the Word to be found in old Puritan volumes, and in later volumes in the same tradition. Another work on the same Epistle which I found valuable and stimulating was that by Adolph Saphir. I remember that I had already found very helpful his *Christ and the Scriptures*, and now I discovered that the fact of his Jewish ancestry gave him an insight into the Epistle to the Hebrews which even Owen, with all his erudition, did not possess. I became increasingly interested in him as a writer when I learned that the Saphir family had been converted to Christ as a result of the enforced detention in Budapest (Hungary), by reason of illness, of two members of the party which left Scotland for the land of Israel in 1839 to enquire, on behalf of the Church of Scotland, into the prospects of opening up an evangelistic work among Jews. The Saphir family consisted of the parents, two sons and three daughters, the children apparently having reached the age of adolescence, the father being over sixty years of age. To the joy of the Scotsmen the entire family believed the gospel, and was joyfully baptised, though not by the missioners, for

the law of the Austro-Hungarian Empire forbade for-
eigners to perform ministerial offices for subjects of the
Hapsburg ruling house. Thereafter it is recorded that the
Saphirs read the New Testament Epistles 'as if they had
arrived by that morning's post'.

I continued in the Sunday School work until my
'worldly' occupation took me from the district. The study
of Hebrews was followed by a survey of Isaiah, except that
between the two I gave lessons on the Five Points of
Calvinism, my first systematic investigation of the doctrines.

4: *A Post in North Wales*

I entered upon my new sphere of experience in the early autumn of 1925. My education had been completed – that is, my formal education, for in other respects education is only terminated by death – by the end of 1924, and I hoped to obtain the kind of post, either administrative or scholastic, where my paper qualifications would find congenial exercise and outlet. But the ensuing months proved a time of very severe testing. My preference was for administration in the educational world, but the Lord did not open the door into such service. Actually I should say re-open, for I had already served three after-school years in a minor capacity in that world. Instead, in the outcome, it was proved beyond a doubt to me that it was his will for me to enter the teaching profession. I had graduated in Manchester in 1923 (a second degree following in late 1924 upon the writing of a thesis on certain aspects of Irish history), and I had seen great cause for thanksgiving in what I could not for a moment doubt was the divine, rather than the human, direction of my studies. From time to time the Lord had given me 'tokens for good' as I pursued my academic course. To begin with he had intervened to change my idea of the chief subject I should pursue, and at several stages of my course he had confirmed not my, but his choice. In my school-days I had paid little attention to History, being somewhat more attracted to scientific subjects. A senior mistress had suggested to me that I should consider entry into the medical profession. On the other hand, at a much later date a university professor recommended me to enter the legal profession. I fear that the method of teaching History at school level was not ideal, for the schoolboy was expected to memorise large numbers of bare facts with a minimum of explanation, and in my school-days it was expected that he should cover practically the whole range of British history in this way. Possibly it was these things that gave me a bias against the subject. Yet in the overruling kindness of God, and in his foreknowledge of things future as well as of things present, I ultimately assented whole-heartedly to the pursuit of historical studies. Indeed, after a spell of preliminary studies in other branches of the Arts, I was invited by the Department of History at the Victoria University of Manchester to follow its Honours course in that subject.

It soon became a source of joy to me to find that historical studies were so eminently suited to a student with the Christian experience and background that was now mine. At so many points a course of General History ran parallel with the long history of Christianity and the church. Mercifully I possessed a retentive memory, though even so I found it taxed to the utmost when for Final Examinations it was necessary to revise virtually the whole of three or more years' work, and focus it, as it were, upon the answering of a series of question papers following rapidly one after another. However the Lord was my Helper. He had given me token after token from his Word that he was interested in furthering my studies, and that it was his purpose to bring them to a successful conclusion. Yet 'conclusion' is doubtless a quite unsuitable word in this context, for a student of History is engaged in an endless task. In truth he must always remain a student.

There is much truth in the view that the student of History, if and when he becomes a teacher of History, must set about the task of learning his subject again, almost as if 'from scratch'. Looked at from one angle, university studies, even those pursued 'in depth' and particularly those involving much memory work, can prove very superficial. 'Cramming' is a temptation ever at hand. In my own case I can turn today to notebooks made with diligent care in the long ago, and it is as though I had never known the facts they contain. But the work of the teacher, if conscientiously performed, leads to knowledge becoming almost ineradicable, that is to say, within reasonable limits. If in any individual case it is not so, pupils quickly conclude that a master is not worth his salt. The teacher is himself subject to the intelligent scrutiny of thirty or perhaps forty pairs of eyes in each of a number of classes. His idiosyncrasies, his weaknesses, his principles, his level of honesty of speech, his degree of skill and knowledge, are readily and accurately perceived by the unconsciously analytical minds of a younger generation, and woe betide him if in their view he is a fit subject for contempt!

In the far-off days to which I refer it was not deemed by any means essential for a person to follow a course of professional training prior to entry into the teaching profession, and my own personal circumstances suggested the wisdom of immediate entry upon a teaching post. But such a post was not easy to obtain. My services became available at a period when a host of other students whose work had been temporarily suspended by World War I were similarly seeking situations. My patience sustained a very severe test, so much so that the day arrived when I virtually told myself that probably the Lord did not intend me to enter the teaching profession. It almost seemed as if he had forgotten to be gracious, and that in anger he had shut up his tender mercies; almost as if he had shut out my prayer, not to say the prayers of my close Christian friends. I refrain from entering into details, though they involved deep spiritual exercises. But I was neither the first nor the last to enter into such an experience.

Finally, almost in desperation, my so-helpful friends, Mr and Mrs Frank Yarwood (both of them now with the Lord) whose eldest daughter Miriam – they had six children – had been my fiancée for several years, decided, with my appreciative consent, that a special family session of confession, humiliation and prayer must be held. It was so held. The ninth chapter of Daniel, in which the prophet confesses the sin of his nation as though it were his own sin, and in which he earnestly prays God to have mercy on his heritage and his people, and to bring to an end their captivity according to his promise and purpose, was read with close attention, and taken to heart. Earnest prayer was offered. All the children of the family were present together with the parents and myself. The following morning a letter reached me from North Wales. It must have been posted before the prayer-session was held – not that that presented any difficulty to us in tracing it to the hand of the Lord – and it was the Lord's answer to our request. It invited me to attend for interview in connection with a post as History Master in the Grammar School at Rhyl. Perhaps I should explain at this point that I had already had about a dozen interviews in different parts of the land for similar vacancies, but without success. But the praying party was on this occasion specially alert to its significance. I duly appeared before the governing body, met with their approval, and shortly entered upon the occupation of a post which remained unchanged (except for promotion) until the day of my retirement from the teaching profession thirty-five years later. It was a post that suited me 'down to the ground'. 'They shall not be ashamed that wait for me' (*Isa. 49:23*). 'Before they call, I will answer; and while they are yet speaking, I will hear' (*Isa. 65:24*). 'At the beginning of thy supplications the commandment came forth' (*Dan. 9:23*). I learned later that the governors of the school were hoping to be able to appoint a Mistress rather than a Master, and that 125 applications for the post had been received. A favoured lady had been invited for interview but she withdrew her application. It was a door opened to me of the Lord, and the years that followed, though not without sundry trials, held much of happiness for me, and I trust, usefulness. A year after appointment came my marriage, a benison from the Lord, and thus a new double chapter opened in my life.

During the year that preceded marriage I occupied 'rooms' and, professionally, I devoted myself to mastering the technique of imparting knowledge, training the mind of youth, and performing such tasks as fell to my lot. I may mention that, from the outset, they included the management of the school library, a rather grandiose term for a collection of perhaps 250 books contained in a very small bookcase. But the office offered scope and I used it to the full. It was quite after my own heart. I should explain that during the previous year and a half I had held two temporary teaching posts, so that when I entered upon work in North Wales I was not a complete novice. The two posts had enabled a shy and awkward young man to accustom himself to the climate of school education and to work off some of his inhibitions. The pleasure of teaching increased rapidly as I attained greater efficiency and became 'more sure of myself', until it merged into a joy that rose superior to the various trials that inevitably intrude upon the chequered pathway of life. The school where I served contained about 150 boys and girls. When I retired from service the number had risen to approximately 750, the sixth form alone, for which I had long been responsible, containing some 120 members. But it is to matters spiritual that I now turn and on which I wish to concentrate.

The first fact that I must record is that in the whole of Wales in 1925 there was but one Strict Baptist Chapel, and that was in Cardiff. It was clear to me therefore that unless I was the means of establishing such a chapel where I was living – and of that there was little likelihood – I should be bereft of Christian fellowship of the type that I had known. But the prospect was not as black as gloomy thoughts suggested, for the Lord is well able to raise up 'children to Abraham' even from stones. I believed this and soon saw evidence of it. When I took my journey into Wales at the first I had received help from words which also became petition: 'Let the blessing come upon the head . . . , and upon the top of the head of him that is separated from his brethren' (*Deut. 33:16*). The words gave me renewed confidence and I used them frequently in prayer.

I was greatly exercised, and especially on the Lord's Days, about a place of worship to which I might turn. I did not know a soul in the place when I arrived but quickly discovered that all the major denominations were represented, and in some cases duplicated because of the language problem. I had high hopes that Wales was in a better state spiritually than was England. I had read of the vast blessings that had come to the Principality in the days of Howel Harris, Daniel Rowland, William Williams (Pantycelyn) and Thomas Charles, and of the extension of those blessings well into the nineteenth century through such ministries as were exercised by Christmas Evans and John Elias, and for all I knew to the contrary, the benefits and benefactions of those ministries continued. Thus I entertained hopes; but I soon discovered that my expectations of fellowship with such, for example, as professed to be Calvinistic Methodists were vain. First of all there was the language barrier. But there was a far greater difficulty. I was soon to learn that modernism in doctrine, and in attitude to the Scriptures, had taken deep root even among those who inherited the traditions of eighteenth-century Methodism. Some, too, I discovered, were what I can only term drama-mad. One of my school colleagues attended a Welsh chapel in the mornings and an English chapel in the evenings on Sundays. I attended the evening service and was invited to supper at his home. 'Is the minister a modernist?' I asked him, for my suspicions had been aroused in the course of the sermon. 'To his fingertips' was the answer I received. My host himself, I was soon to find, held what appeared to me to be very loose views about doctrine. He was unable to say that he believed in the resurrection of Christ from the dead. His reading was more akin to that of the *Hibbert Journal* than of evangelical books of the old school. So my early hopes were quickly dashed. I attended services in several other chapels. In one case I found myself crossing swords with a minister – incidentally, he was a member of the school governing body – who had preached a sermon on 'spiritualism' and had taken the line that, for folk of a certain temperament, the dabbling in the occult was not harmful. I had not heard the sermon, but it had been reported in the local press.

I continued therefore to pray for the Lord's guidance, and the more so as I found that, in Wales, with its ardour for education for the masses, a schoolmaster, by virtue of his profession, was something of a public figure. In fact a report which shortly reached my ears told me that according to hearsay 'a Christian' had joined the staff of the Grammar School. Possibly the rumour gained strength from the fact that the Headmaster had arranged for me to teach Scripture to two or three classes, in addition to my work in History. I had offered Divinity as one of several subsidiary subjects for teaching purposes, and he had taken the word to indicate that I was an

Anglican. He was chagrined to learn that my 'churchman-ship' related to Baptists, not to the Establishment, or rather, to the recently disestablished Church of Wales. It soon appeared that he did not approve of my 'old-fashioned' approach to Scripture, for later he gave the Scripture work to another. But at a later date I returned to it.

I was resident in North Wales three or four weeks before making any advance in respect of my problem of fellowship and worship. Then came a Lord's Day which became almost a red-letter day in my life. I awoke from sleep with a prayer in my heart and probably on my lips also: 'Lead me to the house of my Master's brethren'. I give 'Master's' the capital letter (unlike Genesis 24:27) for an obvious reason. I rarely had the coveted experience of awakening prayerfully. It was not the case that my prayer was prompted by a recent reading of Genesis chapter 24, for I had been reading elsewhere in the Word. But the prayer was accompanied by two convictions, first, that this prayer had been put into my heart by the Lord and no other, second, that he would answer the prayer that selfsame day. I arose hopefully, went to morning worship in a chapel not before visited, and returned to my rooms disappointed. My hopes were now pinned to the evening service, but I was perplexed to know where to attend. Finally, in a measure of desperation, I resolved to attend an Anglican service. The town possessed four Anglican churches, one holding services in Welsh. I thought it perhaps best to go to the most distant of them, and left my rooms in sufficient time to allow for a walk of about two miles. My journey led me through one of the main streets of the town. As I passed along a thoroughfare of shop premises, with residential upper rooms, a notice board caught my eye. It announced the preaching of the Word at, I think, the normal hour of 6.30. Attracted, I opened the door, which was ajar, and exchanged a few words with an elderly person who seemed to be awaiting his friends. My impression, even though the words exchanged were few, was distinctly favourable, and at the appointed time I returned for the service.

This event proved to be my introduction to believers known to the world as Plymouth Brethren. I had heard of them, of course – who had not? – but my Strict Baptist friends had given me to understand that, though they might well be classed as believers in Christ, they held certain peculiar doctrines, and in any event were themselves hostile to all others in Christendom. As yet I knew virtually nothing as to their origin and history and I scarcely knew anything about their notorious deep-rooted contentions and their aptitude for dividing into parties. I soon found it desirable to investigate their origins and their subsequent development. The party where 'my hap' fell proved to be the so-called London party, and I was soon to know that they adhered with the utmost tenacity to the teachings of John Nelson Darby, a second name being that of William Kelly.

I found them locally to be a very friendly and hospitable people. They welcomed me to their meetings, in the hope, no doubt, that I would feel ultimately able to join myself to them. They invited me to their home (their strength lay in one particular family) and were abundantly willing to acquaint me with their doctrines. Ere many days passed I had discovered that, apart from the Scriptures to which they certainly paid the closest attention, they placed very little value on writings other than those which stemmed from their own adherents, that is to say, from about 1830. They had no regard for the great Christian Creeds and Confessions of Faith – probably they had never heard of them – and set aside completely the historical aspects of Christianity. They had practically no interest at all in affairs outside their own small circle. A wide gulf therefore separated me from them, and from the beginning of my contact I sensed that I could never join their fellowship. It possessed a phraseology of its own, it held the various denominations to be in very serious error, it knew nothing of the friendliness which often existed, as I knew, between believers separated by denominational walls; and among its more extreme members there was even the notion that, outside their own ranks, true Christians were not to be found.

Years later I was recommended by a friend to the pages of *Father and Son* by Edmund Gosse, whose father, Philip Henry Gosse, a naturalist of much fame in his day – he specialised in marine biology and wrote several books on his researches – belonged to 'the Brethren', and manifested many of the features of their system of belief and worship. The book is infinitely sad in certain respects, for the son, though he made a profession of faith in Christ, and was baptised, in early adolescence, afterwards turned against his upbringing and seems completely to have set aside all that was of value to his father. I have searched his biography (*Life and Letters of Sir Edmund Gosse*, by Evan Charteris; Heinemann, 1931) for any indication that in his later distinguished career he turned again to the faith of his father, but in vain. He was the premier literary critic of his day, but in his published letters I could not find the vestige of a hope that the Christian faith had re-engaged his heart. In the field of literature his ability was of a very high order and in *Father and Son* he gives a memorable picture of the family and the 'meeting' life of Victorian Brethren which is almost fascinating and certainly enlightening. The subtitle of his book is 'A Study of Two Temperaments'.

As I reflected on the fact of my introduction to the circle of Brethren it was plain matter of fact to me that the Lord had led me amongst them, and that this was the answer to my prayers. I learned thereby that in this far from perfect world the Lord may lead his own to a company in which they may not find their ultimate home on earth, but which is the best in given circumstances. His guidance on a particular occasion may thus prove to be, as time will demonstrate, of an interim character, to be varied at a later date as circumstances and environment change. We are told, for instance, in Acts that, at a certain time, Paul and Silas were 'forbidden of the Holy Ghost to preach the word in Asia' (*Acts 16:6*), but at a subsequent date we find Paul exercising a fruitful ministry in Ephesus, the capital city of that very province.

I learned to appreciate the deep sincerity of my new friends, their genuine spirituality, their unworldly out-look, and their holding forth the Word of the Lord according to their abilities and degree of knowledge. But as I continued in the investigation of their beliefs, both by frequent conversation and by reading, it became increas-ingly evident to me that between certain principles which I had already embraced and principles to which they held as fervently as I to mine, there was no prospect of ultimate reconciliation. My reading of Darby's writings caused me to believe that, to a considerable extent, he held Calvin-istic principles, though not in any historical fashion, but on the other hand I discovered that his views on such subjects as justification were not really related to views held in Reformation days and in later Puritan times. The complete absence of the historical element made his views hard to assess and, I must confess, the obscurity of some of his writings, and their tortuous and peculiar phraseology, added to the difficulty. But in one respect I found myself 'at home' in his teachings. He held that man's will is so perverted that he cannot even 'will to be saved'. I read that, at a meeting between Darby and D. L. Moody, the two men were at cross purposes on this issue, Moody leaning in the direction of free will, and that the dispute became so heated that Darby closed his Bible and refused to proceed.

I give two special instances of the views held by Darby which cut clean across my own. Darby taught that the church of God dates from the Pentecost of Acts chapter 2, and that believers who died before the descent of the Holy Spirit have no part or lot in the church, but belong to a different and inferior body; that, in fact, their eternal portion, though one of perfect blessedness, is of a lower order than that of post-Pentecostal saints. In other words, the greatest of Old Testament saints has a portion in glory inferior to that of the meanest of New Testament believers; or again, that dispensational differences upon earth are eternally perpetuated. As it is not my purpose to write a theological treatise, I say little more about the matter, but state it I must, for my whole soul revolted against the Darbyite view. In the new Jerusalem of Revelation chapter 21, undeniably a representation in symbol of 'the bride, the Lamb's wife', which means, again undeniably, the church of God in the eternal state, I saw that there was an incorporation of both patriarchs and apostles. If the names of the twelve apostles are found in the foundation, no less are the names of the twelve tribes of Israel engraven upon the gates of pearl; Old Testament and New Testament are brought together in the closest harmony and in indissoluble unity. In this and other ways I came to the firm conclusion that Darby and his followers seriously misinterpreted the Scriptures, particularly in the case of some of the Pauline Epistles.

My second instance of differing views relates to church order and government. Darby taught that the church is in ruins, that it has been in ruins in fact since the second century if not earlier, and that it has not been possible, since that ruin set in, to apply the principles of church order detailed for us in the New Testament and in the Epistles in particular. Hence there can be no appointment of elders and deacons, or even of pastors and evangelists. All becomes, as it were, fluid. Men are raised up of God, certainly, but they carry no titles of office. Hence the organisation, such as it is, of Darbyite assemblies is very different from that of, say, the normal Nonconformist church. I confess that it struck me as very strange teaching to claim that the New Testament church order found chiefly in the Epistles was so soon rendered useless and inoperative. Yet so Darby taught. As for baptism, it was made little of, and was often practised, especially in the case of the very young, in the domestic bathroom.

Furthermore, as time went on, I found it needful to investigate the tragic divisions which had taken place within the Brethren movement itself. My friends belonged to the Exclusive section, being commonly known as the Exclusive Brethren. I learned that in an opposing camp were the Open Brethren, and I also read the history of the lamentable contentions that brought about their separation in or about 1848. W. Blair Neatby's *History of the Plymouth Brethren* (Hodder and Stoughton, 1901), of which with difficulty I obtained a copy, was illuminating. The Exclusive section complained that it had a bias in favour of the Open section, but I had reason to think that it gave a fair presentation of the facts of the whole sad story. At the same time I learned to admire greatly the Christianity of such men as Anthony Norris Groves, whose biography I later read with much profit and pleasure, Henry Craik and George Müller, pastor-colleagues at Bethesda, Bristol, and Benjamin Wills Newton who, after the events of 1848, worked on more or less independent lines and produced writings of outstanding worth. In these respects my introduction to the Brethren movement led me to an entirely new field of knowledge.

[51]

For almost a year I attended the Lord's Day meetings of the Exclusive Brethren. In their morning meeting, dedicated to the observance of the Lord's Supper, I 'sat behind' and took no part, except to join in the singing of the hymns. The occasion was marked by great informality, even though it inevitably and invariably followed a certain pattern. It was definitely not intended to be an occasion for 'the ministry of the Word', though all was supposedly based upon the Word. Nor did the praying take the form of petition. It was intended to be a simple act of remembrance of the Lord and his death, and I must confess that I often enjoyed the sheer simplicity and sincerity of what was done. Then came my marriage, and our taking up residence in a village some five miles from school and meeting room. We had a conscience against the use of public transport on the Lord's Day, so we used to walk or occasionally cycle to and from the 'meeting room'. But after a time a new factor came into operation, and our links with Exclusive Brethren and attendance at their gatherings were terminated. I must explain also that my wife's introduction to meetings of a type to which she had not been accustomed was not altogether welcome to her. She tended to look at things which divided us from, rather than those which tied us to, the Brethren.

Some time after our departure from them we learned that developments within their ranks (national, not local) caused our local friends immense trouble and searching of heart. In or about 1930 they had, for the first time, to grapple with the problem that their Central Oversight (an unofficial but highly influential body) required them to repudiate the doctrine of the eternal Sonship of Christ. The practical test which indicated acceptance or rejection of the new doctrine was linked with their *Little Flock Hymnbook*, duly revised according to the decisions of the

Oversight, all references to the eternity of the Lord's Sonship being expunged. With the utmost reluctance our friends gave way to the demands, and so remained within the terms of fellowship of the 'London party'. Twenty years later another crisis blew up. This time the Oversight decreed that it was in order to pray to the Holy Spirit, a thing which had not previously been considered orthodox. Again there was a revision of the hymn-book and again deep searching of heart on the part of our friends. On this occasion they declined to fall into line. Their excommunication *en bloc* followed. Actually, what I can best term their external relations had always been tenuous in character, and they had always conducted themselves, within limits, as a local self-governing unit, so that they continued to hold on their way. Over later developments within the Exclusive body I draw a curtain. They form part of the history of scandal, brought to public notice by the popular newspaper press.

But one thing I would add – that, to my knowledge, the devastation that came to Exclusive Brethren assemblies in the 'sixties of the present century proved for many individuals to be an act of emancipation, for it revealed to them at least three great facts – that their own cherished 'body' was subject to corruption and decay, that true believers in Christ were to be found within the formerly-despised and denounced denominations, and that edifying ministry of the Word was to be met with in quarters which had previously been far removed from their sight, and more wonderful still, even when that ministry was heard from the lips of men who wore a frowned-on type of collar. Not unwisely did a great secular writer say,

> *There is some soul of goodness in things evil,*
> *Would men observingly distil it out.*

[53]

I trust the reader does not construe these words as constituting an attack on the doctrine of 'total depravity'. It is not so, but a worldly man's way of saying that 'all things work together for good to them that love God'.

5: *Favourite Titles in the Beginnings of my Library*

At this point in my narrative I pause in order to make brief reference to some of the books which, supplementary to Scripture but by no means a substitute for it, helped me in my Christian career. Conscious as I am of the wise man's verdict that 'of making many books' – good, bad and indifferent – 'there is no end', and that, accordingly, it is easily possible to waste much valuable time in reading inferior works, I am thankful that, by the Spirit's leading, and in the second place by the guidance of wise friends, my interest was drawn to writings of real worth. My profitable reading commenced about 1919. Up to that year my reading (apart from that already indicated) was desultory and often trivial. I had but feeble discretion to distinguish, in spiritual things, between 'the precious and the vile', between the salutary and the hurtful, between the book faithful to the Word of God and that astray from it.

My conversion introduced me to a new world of books. It would be true to say that my reading was converted as well as my mind and soul. There was little opportunity for reading during my year of service in the Forces, but in any case at that time I was still as a child in things spiritual, hardly able to distinguish between my right hand and my left. My kit-bag contained sundry books which deservedly might well be termed 'impedimenta', for during marches from one camp to another, especially in the Boulogne area and down as far as the Somme, they were almost more than I could shoulder; but they related to matters of secular learning and were remote from spiritual interests.

My Strict Baptist friends, though not my most intimate ones, introduced me early to the writings of J. C. Philpot, and especially such sermons of his as 'Winter afore Harvest' and 'The Heir of Heaven Walking in Darkness and the Heir of Hell Walking in Light'. These and other sermons were 'searching', but I confess frankly that I did not find them, in my then condition of 'seeking', particularly helpful. There was a gloom and a severity linked with them that kept me at bay. Their tendency was to cause the reader to inquire, 'Is it possible for anyone at all to be a Christian?' They were inclined to produce excessive introspection, and although I realised that it was imperative at times to look within and to weigh one's evidences of life, so that the wickedness, the instability and the ungodliness of the 'natural man' might be known, I realised also that growth in grace and in the knowledge of Christ did not consist exclusively in increased knowledge of one's own nature. There were those in church prayer-meetings who not infrequently referred to and sometimes quoted the words of Ezekiel, 'Turn thee yet again and thou shalt see greater abominations than these' (8:15), and one church member in particular was extremely fond of giving us his own interpretation of the words (in very much the same spiritual context), 'What will ye see in the Shulamite? As it were the company of two armies' (*Song of Sol. 6:13*). So I early learned that to bear fruit upward it was urgently needful to take root downward (*Isa. 37:31*). On the other hand I genuinely felt that the trend of true Christianity was towards joy and light 'in the Lord' rather than towards gloom and darkness. Philpot seemed to preach so much about the gloomier side of Christian experience! At times, too, in my immature view, he seemed to use scriptural texts, especially from the prophets, for purposes which appeared very remote from what I took to be their true and original meaning.

I mention Philpot at some little length because he was so highly esteemed among my Baptist friends. His word and outlook 'went a long way with them'. I desire to be perfectly fair to his type of ministry. I recollect that in later years, when I had some contact with a pastor-evangelist among Open Brethren, he told me that he revelled in the sermons. I suspect that he found them an antidote to the superficiality which often disfigured the 'profession of the Lord' in quarters where he moved. I do not doubt that I received benefit from Philpot's works, so far as I knew them. In later years I very much admired his handling of the doctrine of Christ's eternal Sonship in his book on that vitally important subject. In general I valued his books other than his sermons. All in all there was a weightiness about his words which was impressive, and his sound classical scholarship (he had been Fellow of Worcester College, Oxford, but resigned his Fellowship for spiritual reasons in a letter of great forcefulness) appealed to me. I was later to find his son Dr J. H. Philpot's *Seceder* volumes very attractive reading. From them I quote words of this preacher which appear on the back of the title page of Volume I:

> I stand before Him, Whose eyes are as flames of fire, to search out the secrets of my heart. And what is this poor vain world with all its gilded-clay, painted-touchwood honours and respectability, and soap-bubble charms? What is all the wealth of the Church piled up in one heap, compared to a smile of a loving Saviour's countenance?

Words which in their turn remind me of the last lines of verse that Charles Wesley ever wrote:

> *O could I catch one smile from Thee,*
> *And drop into eternity!*

Men who could write such words knew not a little of 'the loveliness of Christ'.

After Philpot who, after all, at the beginning of my Christian career did not engage too much of my attention, I mention Elisha Coles and his work on *The Sovereignty of God* which I read in an old shabby copy still in my possession. In recent years it was reprinted in a series of small pamphlets by the Sovereign Grace Union, though doubtless in popular favour it has now been largely replaced by Pink's book under the same title. Coles, a Puritan, died in 1680. He is best known to the secular world as a lexicographer and stenographer (that is, as a dictionary-maker and an inventor of an old form of shorthand), but for the Christian his title to fame rests on his book just named. It is a sturdy, clear and plain analysis of its subject with an abundance of biblical illustration. In its day it was strongly recommended for popular reading by several eminent Puritans including John Owen. From its pages I was confirmed in my Calvinistic doctrine.

Next I mention Thomas Boston of Ettrick, whose collected works (not quite all of them) I possess in an old folio volume. But it is in the smaller editions of his various works that I find it preferable to read. My interest in Boston is such that when I took my first journey into Scotland, or at least one of my early journeys, I paid a visit to the out-of-the-way Ettrick, called at its manse, was shown a large chest containing Boston relics including the ancient church records written in Boston's own hand, and of course visited the church building itself, furnished as it seemed to me so awkwardly, where the good man ministered gloriously from 1707 to 1732. His *Fourfold State* (man in a state of innocence, man in a state of nature, man in a state of grace, and man in a state of glory) impressed me greatly, and only a little less so his work on *The Crook in the Lot*, and his *Soliloquy on the Art of Man-Fishing*. Equally, if not even more prized by me, is a volume which 'came my way' (as I find) in 1923, entitled *Memoirs of . . . Thomas Boston, Divided into Twelve Periods, Written by Himself and Addressed to his Children*. It was published in 1776, that is, forty-four years after his death. On the blank fly-leaves at the back of the book I find that at the time of my reading it I made no less than eighty-one references to topics mentioned, including such matters as 'the manner of proclaiming the Gospel', 'the mystery of Christ in the form of a servant', 'sin in the regenerate', 'absolute God', 'quaint remark on heaven', 'his poor opinion of himself', and so on. As soon as time permits I must re-read the volume for my good. So from Boston I must have gleaned more lessons than now I am conscious of, after half a century of time. My personal 'everyday book' (for I have kept one for not a few years) contains, I find, the following quotation from the *Memoirs*;

> Singing at family worship Psalm 121, this view of the Bible was given me, viz: that whatever were the particular occasions of the writing of it, or any part thereof, I am to look upon it as written for me as much as if there were not another person in the world, and so is everybody to whose hand it comes.

What else can I add to this but 'Let every reader say Amen'?

Linked closely with my memories of Boston are recollections of the great value I derived from my reading of *The Marrow of Modern Divinity* by Edward Fisher. Were a book to be published under the same title today it might well be regarded with the greatest suspicion by evangelicals. But Fisher's book is a Godsend. It was the book that sparked off the famous Marrow Controversy in the Church of Scotland in and after 1717. Boston was serving in Simprin parish before he went to Ettrick. A Scottish soldier who had served in the wars of the Commonwealth period in England brought it back to Scotland and kept it on his cottage bookshelf. Boston borrowed it and was tremendously impressed by its contents. The date of its first publication was 1645–9, by which time apparently some were advocating a 'close' in preference to an 'open' gospel, that is to say, close or open as far as the proclamation of the gospel was concerned. The book consists of a series of dialogues, with numerous excerpts from standard divines, especially those of Puritan persuasion. Boston, sensing that the book's thrust would be beneficial in his own day, introduced it to others, and ere long 'Marrow-men' found themselves in heated controversy with men of narrower views. It became a tug of war between 'Marrow-men' and narrow men. The work was influential for good. It was reprinted in a modern format, edited by Dr C. G. M'Crie, in 1902. I read the book in an old copy of 1781 (including Notes by Boston) while on holiday on the east coast of Anglesey in the summer of 1923, and found it, as a very scanty record reminds me, 'highly edifying and instructive: some things in it are hard to be understood'.

I close my all-too-brief record of the value of Thomas Boston and *The Marrow* by mentioning that, in the 'twenties, a Christian in Camberwell warned me that *The Fourfold State* was full of free-will teaching. I thought at that time that probably the winds of Hyper-Calvinism had been blowing over that London suburb. Not that Henry Atherton was their source! Through lack of knowledge I leave the matter unresolved.

About the year 1923 I found myself supplied with, and

reading, the biographies of several Strict Baptist ministers, chiefly Daniel Smart of Cranbrook, Kent, Thomas
Godwin whose place of ministry I forget, Francis Kirby of
Ramsgate, Eli Ashdown of Sussex and London, John
Kershaw of Rochdale, John Warburton of Trowbridge,
Francis Covell of Croydon, and a certain Mr James
Turton of South Lancashire whose tribute to sovereign
grace he termed his 'Pillar'. These biographies – one or
two are autobiographies – contained many points of
interest, and here and there were 'more than interesting';
so I began the habit of keeping a book of short extracts,
later finding that it was essential to keep it indexed,
otherwise it lost some of its usefulness. I have found such a
book extremely valuable for a variety of purposes.

A book of special importance that reached me during
this formative period of my life was *Calvin's Institutes*, not
however the complete work the size of which is, after all,
forbidding for a beginner, but an abridgement (quite
recently re-published) made by a Cambridge scholar. The
Institutes have appeared over the years in all sorts of shapes
and sizes. Among my 'treasures' is a vellum-bound folio
copy of the Latin version dated 1617. I confess that I
rarely consult it. On the other hand, as I write, I am
looking at a copy measuring three inches by five, the title
page of which states that it had been 'condensed into
Latin' by 'Master William Lawne' (1583) and 'translated
into English by Christopher Fetherstone' (1586). There
have been various translations including one of very
recent date. The Cambridge scholar I mention was Joseph
Pitts Wiles (a former Foundation Scholar of Trinity
College) who became Strict Baptist minister at Devizes,
Wiltshire. Somehow or other I came into touch with him
by letter in 1923 and he presented me with a copy of his
translation in the title of which he used the term
'Instruction' instead of 'Institutes'. It met my need of

systematic instruction in the Christian faith admirably, being a mere 196 pages instead of the 1,200 and more pages of the complete work. It extracts the most basic and profitable parts of the *Institutes* for the general reader, presents them in excellent and forceful English, and provides a first-rate introduction to the Protestant theology, biblically based, which stems from the Reformation. I soon began to realise that Calvin's work is perhaps the greatest book of Christian theology that European Christendom has known.

I also used to receive a monthly printed sermon from Mr Wiles, but it was his book that served me best. He also published *Half-hours with Isaiah*, and *Half-hours with the Minor Prophets* which served me as an introduction to those Books and which I found helpful, the more so as I admired the purity of his English style. Thus his own rendering of Isaiah 23:16 was as follows:

> *Forgotten harlot, take thine harp,*
> *And ply thy trade again;*
> *Fill every street with sweetest song,*
> *And win thee back thy men.*

– a sad theme, but the melodious lines eminently suited it!

As yet I had barely made contact with the more famous of the Puritans. The volumes of Sibbes and Thomas Goodwin (the excellent reprints in the Nichol series) were appearing on my horizon, but it was some time before I dipped into them. With William Perkins too I had slight acquaintance and his three folio volumes of 1617 are with me still. John Owen I have already briefly mentioned. I seem to remember that it was the Stephen Charnock volumes (Nichol series) which, in this class of works, appealed to me most. Portions of his work on the divine attributes were impressive and rich, and I found equally good material also in his sermons on the sacrificial work of

Christ. He seemed to have a wonderful facility in quoting texts and words and phrases from all parts of the Scriptures in illustration of any theme he was handling. Of course, this applies in measure to all the Puritans, but Charnock seemed to excel them all in this way.

Amid all the wealth of material which opened to my vision, I need make no attempt to defend the statement that, understandably, it was the writings of John Bunyan which had the strongest appeal. Christian classics never really conflict one with another. They serve the cause of the one Master,

> *Flashing back the noonday light,*
> *Rank behind rank, like surges bright,*
> *Of a broad sea of gold.*

In Bunyan's case, his *Grace Abounding to the Chief of Sinners*, his *Pilgrim's Progress*, and his *Holy War* were the precise pabulum that my soul needed, and these works were read by me, probably with more pleasure, in the usual sense of that word, than most of the other works I have mentioned. Maybe it was because the tinker's literary style, though not exalted or scholarly, was charming and gripping. I discovered that 'this private under Fairfax, this minister of God' possessed a genius which came to him neither by education nor from any other quarter, but was the sheer sovereign gift of God. But without conversion it would never have been! His literary style, while in a sense non-literary, was all that could be desired by a young believer. In his writings, therefore, the 'going was good'. He knew how to present the deepest truth in pleasant form, to get truth into head and heart before the reader was aware of his artfulness, to hit nails on their heads, to deal shrewd blows at all errors that dared raise their heads, and, in sum, to cast a glory around the presentation of saving truth that proved him a worthy son of the Master whose he was and whom he served. My only regret as I pored over his writings was that time was insufficient to assimilate so much they contained that so well deserved assimilation.

To the above-named works I must add Bunyan's *Life and Death of Mr Badman*. Of Badman Bunyan wrote: 'His religion hangs by in his house as his cloak does, and he seldom in it except he be abroad'. And further I was impressed by the words (in reference to Matthew 5:28): 'He that would steal doth steal; he that would cheat doth cheat; he that would swear doth swear . . . As a man thinketh, so is he'. I am tempted to quote much more extensively, but I forbear. Yet I venture to include two verdicts on Bunyan by men of discernment:

> Prick Bunyan anywhere and you will find that his blood is Bibline.
>
> (Spurgeon)

> Bunyan: one of the most fertile geniuses the world ever produced.
>
> (Archibald Alexander)

Who could not but learn from such a man?

My next tribute must be paid to George Whitefield even though his genius did not find expression by means of the pen but by use of the tongue. I had heard little of his fame in my Methodist days, a silence not hard to be understood in a Wesleyan environment, but among Strict Baptists he was a star of the first magnitude in the firmament of preachers. Actually I think it would be fair to say that many Strict Baptists believed in his fame and held high his reputation while they remained substantially ignorant of his printed sermons, for in certain cases they would have classed him, alas, in his free proclamation of the gospel, among the 'free-willers'. But where better judgment prevailed, he was indeed highly esteemed. Probably it was his biography even more than his sermons which appealed to me in those early days. One's feelings were stirred to their depths by accounts of the preachings in Moorfields, London, at Kingswood, Bristol, and in scores of other places at home and abroad. My introduction to the preacher was actually made through a Scottish volume (edited by the Rev D. Macfarlan and published in 1845) which narrated the results of Whitefield's visit to Scottish revival scenes, especially at Cambuslang. Appended to the narrative are three sermons preached by Whitefield in the Highchurchyard, Glasgow, and it was the second of these which held my chief interest. Its title was 'The Method of Grace', and its text Jeremiah 6:14 ('They have healed also the hurt . . . saying, Peace, peace; when there is no peace'). In it the preacher traces out the various items of conviction which a sinner must know before he may speak peace to his heart: actual transgressions, original sin that caused the transgressions, the 'splendid sins' of religious duties and performances, unbelief. And on the positive side the sinner must be enabled to lay hold of the perfect all-sufficient righteousness of the Lord Jesus Christ. These matters having been stated at some length Whitefield proceeds to address several sorts of persons and to give appropriate exhortations to each. 'Some of you', he says, 'may think that I carry things too far. But, indeed, when you come to judgment, you will find what I say is true, either to your eternal damnation or comfort. May God influence your hearts to come to him! I am not willing to go away without persuading you . . . go away with full resolution, in the strength of God, to cleave to Christ'. My reading of this sermon, and later of others akin to it, made me thereafter a Whitefield lover. Long afterwards, in an auction, I purchased an eighteenth-century coloured bust of Whitefield – the auctioneer announced that it was one of Wesley – and occasionally look at it with a small degree of veneration (even though it lies in a box in the loft), but it is the sermons and message of the man that have entered my heart: there, being dead, he 'yet speaketh'.

Foxe's Book of Martyrs must receive its due meed of praise. My historical training naturally led to my finding particular pleasure in the reading of what is, undeniably, a major source-book for the history of Tudor England, if of no other periods. I soon came to realise that the original *Foxe* was no small work purchasable for a mere trifle, as some still suppose. Actually it was a folio of considerable thickness; one such came into my possession in later years. In its seventeenth-century editions it consisted of three semi-folio volumes and in the nineteenth century it reappeared in eight thick volumes of somewhat smaller size. Needless to say it contains information that stirs the blood and demonstrates the complete unworthiness of many of us to bear the honoured name of Protestants. To anticipate the findings of later days, I would here say that I was cheered by the writings of J. L. Mozley about 1940 when with great success he defended Foxe as an accurate historian against the charges which certain nineteenth-century writers had levelled at him.

The *Memoirs of Thomas Halyburton* came my way also. I was impressed by the way in which he mourned the sins of his childhood and by the resemblance between his Memoirs and those of Thomas Boston to which I have already referred. The account of the death of his child George drew my special attention, as also did the account of his own death-bed. About the same time I read the autobiography of another Scot, John G. Paton of the New Hebrides, of whom it may now be said that his fame is heard in 'all churches of the saints'. His own graphic account of missionary work among cannibals, and the joy that came to him as, finally, after years of sacrificial service, saved ones were to be seen sitting at the table of the Lord, presents the picture of a man wholly dedicated to the work of the gospel. It is almost a benediction in itself to look at the photograph of the long-bearded, silver-haired hero of Aniwa and Tanna which is found in some editions of his volume. The two Hudson Taylor volumes were read by me also with very great interest and profit. C. H. Spurgeon came into my life at a later date, so my enthusiastic mention of him and his written work must be reserved for a later chapter.

A minor writer whom I found pleasure in reading was Charlotte Elizabeth (Mrs Tonna) whose *Personal Recollections* (partly covering certain aspects of Irish life) I found profitable. A book of quite a different type which I read diligently was Thomas Whitelaw's *How Is the Divinity of Jesus Depicted in the Gospels and Epistles?* (1883), its divisions being 'The Divinity of Jesus in Pre-Existent Glory', in 'Incarnate Self-abasement' and in 'Post-incarnate Exaltation'. It introduced me to some of the problems of that branch of theology.

Incidentally, as I have just mentioned a female writer, I might also mention that my wife derived immense pleasure and benefit from Adelaide L. Newton's small *Commentary on the Song of Songs* (1871). Her biographer described her as a 'living martyr' by reason of ill health. Her book is strikingly true to Reformation doctrine. Spurgeon comments that her 'book is very dear to spiritual minds; it is full of that quiet power which comes from the Spirit of God through deep experience and precious fellowship with the Well-Beloved'. High commendation indeed!

Last but not least – and I wish to give all the emphasis I can to 'not least' – is a work that, when first read by me, lifted my thinking and brought edification to my soul (and I should really say to 'our two souls') as much as, if not much more than, most other volumes. I refer to William Gurnall's *Christian in Complete Armour*. I forget how the book first came to my notice after conversion, although I have mentioned previously that there was a copy on my father's bookshelves, but it meant nothing to me before conversion. I quickly learned after arrival in Wales that, in a Welsh translation, of which I could not estimate the merits, it had been a strong first-favourite with Calvinistic Methodists in the heyday of the eighteenth-century revival, and as I began to turn over its pages I soon realised why this was the case. For the sake of those who know nothing of the book I must explain that it consists of many sermons, all reasonably short – for a Puritan! – on the armour mentioned by Paul in Ephesians chapter 6; but in handling the passage Gurnall (minister of Lavenham in Suffolk from 1644 to 1679) covers most aspects of Christian doctrine, experience and practice in simple and memorable fashion. The work appeared in three volumes between 1655 and 1662 (I possess two of the three in these first editions) and was re-published by a London printer named Tegg in the mid-nineteenth century. But the J. C. Ryle edition of 1864–5 is a vast improvement upon it.

Gurnall is witty, pithy, pointed, interesting, edifying, and much more. His sermons are lightened and enlightened by illustrations drawn from three chief sources – everyday life, country life in special, and ancient history. A typical illustration of the first is that concerning Christian assurance. Gurnall states that many Christians possess assurance without knowing it, just as it is possible for a man to walk around the house looking for his hat when it is upon his head all the time. For the second group I take an illustration concerning the different attitudes of genuine and merely nominal Christians towards divine promises. 'The greyhound', he says, 'hunts by sight. When he cannot see the game he gives over running. But the true hound hunts by scent. He goes over hedge and ditch, though he sees not the hare he pursues all day long. An unbelieving heart, may be, is drawn out, upon some visible probabilities and sensible hopes of a mercy coming to pass; but when these are out of sight, his heart fails him. But faith keeps the scent of the promise, and gives not over the chase.' As for a third illustration taken from ancient history, take the following: 'It was a high piece of ingenuity and clemency in Augustus, that having promised by a proclamation a great sum of money to any that should bring him the head of a famous pirate, did yet, when the pirate, who had heard of this, brought it himself to him, and laid it at his foot, not only pardon him for his former offences against him, but reward him for his great confidence in his mercy.' The application is so obvious that I leave it to the reader.

So much must suffice for my chapter on books that influenced me in the early days of my Christian career. 'For the time would fail me to tell' of the rest. The period dealt with is approximately 1919–27.

6: *Sunday Afternoons in Rhyl*

My last chapter of narrative ended with the remark that
my wife and I knew beyond a doubt that we could never
join the Exclusive Brethren fellowship. We felt in our
bones that there was too great a difference between their
beliefs, in toto, and our own, to render entry into anything
like full fellowship possible. It would doubtless be
possible to agree on various matters, for in the vast
spectrum of Christian truth there were inevitably many
'colours' common to both, but full church fellowship was
not to be contemplated. It would have involved the
cutting off of ourselves from Christians of all other types,
to start with; Strict Baptist friends and fellow-believers,
and indeed all others, for the term 'Exclusive' not only
meant separation from Open Brethren, but also from
believers of every other type; indeed, from various kinds
of Exclusives also, for within the narrow world of
Exclusivism party was ranged against party. The group
containing my friends was the London party and it
regarded with considerable hostility the Raven party, the
Stuart and Kelly parties, and I suppose sundry other
parties too. It is amazing that such animosities should
have persisted down to the present day. I give one
illustration drawn from 'the ends of the earth'. An
undenominational Quarterly of which the present writer
happens to be Editor reached a subscriber of fairly long
standing who was located in a part of far-away Borneo. In
one issue he found an article by Benjamin Wills Newton, a

distinguished member of the early Brethren, one who in fact figured in the disputes of 1848. He was incensed, sent a letter manifesting his displeasure, and withdrew his support of the Quarterly. 'Roots of bitterness' are apt to bear fruit long after the first sowing.

What then was to be the course of action of my wife and myself? Were we to draw into isolation, and weave around ourselves, as it were, threads of gossamer and become, as it were, spiritual cocoons? Were there no other local believers with whom fellowship was possible? I hasten to give John Wesley the credit for a saying of great value: 'Christianity knows nothing of a solitary religion'. Happily, at this point we received guidance, circumstantially, which we believe came from above. A commercial traveller, ready of speech (as his calling rendered desirable), but, better still, a lover of the Lord and his Word, broke away from the local church where he and his family had been in fellowship, his reason for doing so being the modernism which characterised the preaching. In actual fact it was the church whose pastor was a modernist 'to his fingertips'. He, his wife and his family of four young sons, began to hold informal meetings with regularity 'around the Word' in his own house. He bore good testimony, confessing the Lord boldly, and as might be expected of a commercial traveller, tactfully. Unperceived by him he gave me unspoken hints in the sphere of Christian witness. Gradually, too, I came to understand that valuable lessons of Christian behaviour, witness and conduct were to be learned from all other believers who came to play a conspicuous part in one's life; occasionally negative lessons, but normally positive.

Commander Salwey, a noted text-carrier, was the friend of our new acquaintance. On one occasion when for the first time a cinema secured permission from the local authority or the magistrates to open on Sunday evenings, our friend secured a large text of Scripture and paraded up and down the queue outside the cinema, the meanwhile handing out tracts of which he always kept a supply at the ready. On another occasion, when Edward, Prince of Wales (later Edward VIII), arrived for the official opening of a hospital, he prepared in large letters a special text to display in long scroll fashion across the upper part of his house where the Prince and his retinue, together with large crowds, were sure to see it. The words ran 'O God . . . give thy righteousness unto the king's son' (*Psalm 72:1*). On Sunday afternoons he attended at the same hospital, where he had received informal permission to distribute Christian literature and to converse with any who welcomed his friendly approaches.

Following upon his retirement from commercial work, in or about 1936, our friend moved to Scotland and devoted the remainder of his years to evangelistic and colportage work in that land. His removal led me to take up his hospital work, and for the next twenty-five years I was enabled on Sunday afternoons to visit the hospital mentioned, and to add to the service regular visits to a second and very much larger hospital distant little more than half a mile away. The two hospitals served, not their immediate localities only, but most parts of North Wales also. By the kindness of the matrons and staff of the two hospitals I was able to go from bed to bed in the general wards, and to individuals lodged in private wards, in order to engage in conversation with them and with their relations and friends visiting them. It was not always possible to enter into conversation on matters spiritual; one had to listen as well as to speak; but in many cases a few words were possible, and in all cases booklets of Scripture leaflets were given to those who would receive them, in itself a clear indication of the purpose of the visit. I met with few refusals. I recall that one person, a professed atheist, spoke a loud refusal, which caused me to suppose that loudness supplied a substantial part of the argument against God and godliness. Bunyan, I recalled later, tells us that Atheist, on speaking to Christian and Hopeful, 'fell into a very great laughter', and the pilgrim's record runs: 'They turned away from the man [that is, after certain conversation] and he, laughing at them, went his way'. There was bitterness rather than laughter in the reaction of my hospital patient, but the loudness and the laughter were akin.

I was careful to pass on Scripture portions only, for this could not be considered a sectarian work. I made only one exception to this practice and objection was never taken to it. Having come to value greatly the sermons of C. H. Spurgeon, I bought as many volumes as I could find of the *Metropolitan Tabernacle Pulpit*. I built up a set for my own use, but in all I acquired some hundred volumes of duplicates, each containing fifty-two sermons. These I detached from their bindings, and on each visit to the hospitals I took with me some six or seven sermons. Where I found sufficient interest in Christian things to warrant it, and especially in the cases of the odd believer I discovered, I would pass on a sermon with a word of commendation. Over the years I met a great number of people in this hospital fashion. Some were mere birds of passage, here today and gone tomorrow. Others – crippled, diseased, halt, lame, rarely blind, laid low for a while – might be detained a dozen weeks or months. In their cases it was not always easy to pass on a long succession of different Scripture portions, but of these sermons there was virtually no end. The hospitals did not possess chaplains; they were served by local ministers, but their visits were not made on Sunday afternoons, so there were no collisions. As I was a schoolmaster I often met with the parents of children I knew and this was a helpful matter rather than otherwise.

On one occasion I ingratiated myself unexpectedly with a member of Jehovah's Witnesses who was occupying a sick-bed. It happened that a conference for members of school staffs engaged in the teaching of Scripture, whether at primary or secondary level, had been arranged by the County Education Authority, and I attended two or three of its sessions. To my dismay I found that the lecturer, an old Methodist minister of some academic prowess, was most decidedly Higher Critic. He told us, for example, that there was nothing historically reliable in the Old Testament before Joshua (or it may have been Judges), and in the few minutes reserved for questions after the lecture, I raised my protest. I met the member of Jehovah's Witnesses only a few days later, and we entered into conversation about the inspiration of the Scriptures, a theme on which we might expect to find common ground. In the midst of our exchanges, the Witness took pains to tell me of the teachers' conference, and, said he, 'There was only one person there, out of several scores, who protested against what the lecturer had said'. Needless to say, when I revealed the identity of the protester, my stock with the Witness rose rapidly.

Occasionally a conversation was followed by the receipt of a letter from a patient who had returned home. I remember vividly one case where the sufferer was an old man of, I think, at least four-score years – he must have long departed this life – named Hone. I should explain that, in entering upon conversation, I did not usually launch immediately into things spiritual. I had noted that, in the case of the woman at the well (*John, chapter 4*) the Lord in his wisdom (I prefer this word to 'tact' in this case) did not begin his talk with her in a 'religious' way, but with a matter-of-fact request. He approached the spiritual via the natural. 1 Corinthians 15:46, if it is permissible to wrench it out of its context for this purpose, words the matter as exactly as I could wish – 'first that which is natural; afterward that which is spiritual'. I assure my readers that, in a different context still, I most certainly believe that it is a biblical principle of the utmost importance to seek *first* the spiritual (*Matt. 6:33*), and this being done, the natural falls under divine guarantee. But it was the Lord's deliberate practice to lay hold of anything at hand in the natural world that might serve the spiritual end which he had in view; and to do this for women equally with men. 'What man of you . . . either what woman?'

In this case it was the name of Hone that gave me my clue. I had long had an interest in the case of William Hone, the arch-blasphemer of England in the first half of the nineteenth century, who for blasphemous parodies of the Litany, the Athanasian Creed, and the Church of England Catechism had been brought to court. The prosecution was conducted by the Attorney General at the Old Bailey, but Hone was acquitted of having actually broken the law as it stood. Yet in the eyes of evangelicals, if not at the bar of the State, he was held to have a pernicious influence on his fellows. Part of the tragedy was that his father was a Huntingtonian, that is, a follower of William Huntington S. S. (sinner saved) who carried Calvinistic doctrine to an extreme, his ministerial career being marked by 'war to the death' against Arminianism. Several of his works are still highly esteemed, though they need to be read with caution. But the saving feature of William Hone's career was that, in later life, he tasted sovereign grace to the full. He experienced a saving conversion to Christ, repented deeply, and preached the faith which once he destroyed. Many glorified God in him. These things I told, with all necessary brevity, to the Mr Hone whom I faced, and having done so was able to proceed to explain the purpose of my visit. He remained perhaps three weeks in hospital and then I saw him no more. But weeks or months later I had a letter in which for the first time he let me know that he made profession of belief in Christ. Some things in his letter showed much confusion of thought, but ere he closed he quoted the verse of a hymn and told me that it summed up his testimony:

> *In peace let me resign my breath,*
> *And Thy salvation see;*
> *My sins deserve eternal death,*
> *But Jesus died for me.*

I never saw him again. He was not untypical of many who crossed my pathway for a brief moment, listened to a word, received a booklet, and disappeared from my view. 'The day will declare it.'

I met with a very striking case, illustrative of the oft-quoted words, 'Cast thy bread upon the waters: for thou shalt find it after many days' (*Eccles. 11:1*). Though not connected with hospital work it concerned an invalid. A girl came to the school in which I taught, as a transfer from elsewhere. She was the daughter of a foreign consul and she entered directly into the school's sixth form. I did not know it at the time, but later I learned that she was a Roman Catholic. Yet she attended the weekly General Scripture lesson for which I was responsible. She remained two years in school and then entered a university to work for a degree in Music. It was my business to trace the future careers of old pupils, especially those who entered university, and as, after several years, we had heard nothing of her progress and presumed successes, I made inquiries at the university in question, only to learn that she had left after two years and had not proceeded to a degree. All remained a blank for a while, but some twelve or more years later I received a letter from her that made me both joyful and sad. She began by telling me that I would be 'glad to know that my bread cast upon the waters had been found after many days'. Then she went on to say that at university she had wasted her time, drifted into very undesirable company and ways, and broken her mother's heart. Suddenly she had been struck down with multiple sclerosis, but this calamity had been the means used by God to bring her to her senses and, better still, to himself. An ambulance driver, linked with Pentecostalists, who was serving her need, spoke with her, discovered her sad spiritual plight, introduced her to his friends, and as a result she had been translated from the kingdom of darkness into that of God's dear Son. Her sclerosis remained despite the prayers and admonitions of Pentecostalist workers, but her soul was saved.

The letter told me further how she had resented the Scripture lessons and had considered that my upbringing of my sons (who attended the school in which I taught) was too severe! Now all was changed. She believed the Scriptures in a new way and rejoiced in the Lord. I corresponded with her, for she lived at a distance, and she further told me of her belief that the Lord would heal her and send her as a Christian worker among the Jewish people. On several occasions I was able to visit her. But she derived her ideas about healing from her Pentecostal friends, and they proved to be delusive. Ultimately she died at about the age of forty, still an invalid. Her testimony was an encouragement to me to remain 'steadfast, unmoveable, always abounding in the work of the Lord', knowing that such 'labour is not in vain in the Lord'. Yet, at best, we remain 'unprofitable servants'!

Testimony in the hospitals to Roman Catholics presented special problems. I had to be very careful not to go too far, by which I mean that testimony could not be as free as might be the case on other ground. A hospital patient cannot well escape from an unwanted visitor and it was highly undesirable for an interview to end with the Romanist saying 'Please go'. To the best of my recollection, nothing approaching this ever occurred. I did not press conversation upon the unwilling, nor booklets into hostile hands. If the attention of a stranger was at all resented I made no attempt to remain. In any case some patients were too ill to welcome words from the unknown visitor. Certainly one needed much of the 'gentleness of Christ'. Better to say nothing, or next to nothing, than to speak inappropriately or unkindly. Better to pass by a bed, if it was surrounded by relations who considered the stranger to be an intruder. Such matters had to be judged with prudent and prayerful care. But as I look back on my visits I thank the Lord for making them possible; and I may add that when they ceased, on my leaving Wales, and could not be resumed in the new area of residence, I often looked back upon them nostalgically and longed for their recurrence. Time inevitably brings its changes. Opportunities are to be 'bought up' as and when they occur. 'The night cometh when no man can work.' One must 'walk' and work while it is day.

A further reference to the case of William Hone will perhaps interest readers as much as that case interested myself. I have mentioned Hone's notorious career. A hint or two as to how he turned to be a renegade may be a guide as to how not to bring up children. Mention afterwards as to how he became a believer will produce a balance.

As I have said, Hone's father was a Huntingtonian. Unhappily it was a characteristic of this strongly Calvinistic body to despise and speak with great harshness about Arminians. John Wesley in particular they spoke of with great bitterness. To them he was the apostle of error. They were even prepared to call him a 'child of the devil'. As a boy William Hone attended an old-dame school, even though, strange as the case may seem, the proprietress was a member of the Wesleyan body. Hone was one of her favourite pupils. She was taken ill. The boy was given the special privilege of visiting her. As he did so on one occasion, the maid came into the bedroom to announce a visitor. It was none other than John Wesley in old age. The boy sitting by the bedside was at once thoroughly alarmed, for was not Wesley 'a child of the devil'? The boy gazed in terror and wonder. There entered a venerable old man, his silvered hair hanging down to his shoulders, his complexion fresh and placid, his smile sweet. To the boy's amazement he seemed to have the countenance of an angel. He ministered to the lady, spoke comforting words, knelt down, prayed, and took his departure, saying to the awe-struck lad as he did so, 'God bless you, my child, and make you a good man'. In later years Hone passed this comment: 'I never saw Mr Wesley again; my dame died; but from that hour I never believed anything my father said, or anything I heard at chapel. I felt, though I could not have expressed it, how wicked was such enmity between Christians; and so I lost all confidence in my good father and in all his religious friends, and in all religion'.

A lesson here on how not to speak about one's theological adversaries, and, above all, in the home!

A second happening which aroused the boy's resentment was a common form of discipline exercised by the father. I quote Hone's own words: 'The ordinary penance for a slight fault was to get by heart a chapter of the Bible. Once, being set such a task, sitting on the garret stairs, I threw the book down the whole flight, saying, "When I am my own master I will never open you". Thereafter for thirty years I never looked into the Bible.'

But now to mention of his conversion! I confine the account to two factors which operated to produce it. One was a dream. He dreamt that he visited a certain house,

[79]

and as the person whom he wished to see was not immediately available he had to wait for a short while. In the room where he sat he noted a window shutter of apparently unusual design, and in the wooden frame of the shutter he further noticed a knot of singular appearance. Some time later, during a visit to the country, he entered a house never before visited by him, and to his amazement he was in the room of his dream. Fascinated he turned to the window and found the shutter of his dream, and there too was the knot in the wood. As he reflected on the happening his cherished theories of materialism were overthrown. He received the firm conviction that there must exist spiritual agencies as susceptible of proof as any facts of physical science. This proved to be one of the links in a chain of events which God used for his conversion, for it caused him, as he said, 'to bow to an unseen and divine power, and ultimately to believe and live'.

The second link I mention concerns Wales, and is of the simplest possible type. Hone was on a riding holiday in Wales. At a rural cottage door he paused to make an inquiry or to seek refreshment, and spoke to a young girl sitting in the doorway reading a book. To his considerable surprise he learned that the book in which the girl was so absorbed was the Bible. She told him that it was her chief joy when her duties for the day were completed to read the sacred Book. He told her next that he supposed it must be her 'task' so to do. He could hardly believe his ears when she earnestly assured him to the contrary. For the first time in his life he saw that a Bible could be a source of the greatest pleasure, and that, even to the young! It set him upon a course of hard thinking, and contributed to the conversion which amazed all his contemporaries.

I close with verses which Hone composed to commemorate his conversion. After some thirty years – for I met with them first in 1939 – they still remain with me as an inspiration:

> *The proudest heart that ever beat*
> *   Has been subdued in me:*
> *The wildest will that ever rose*
> *To scorn Thy cause or aid Thy foes,*
> *   Is quelled, my God, by Thee.*
>
> *Most glorious Saviour, here I see*
> *   A trophy of Thy grace,*
> *Such as should ever silence those*
> *Who would Thy Majesty oppose,*
> *   And dare Thee to Thy face.*
>
> *Thy will and not my will be done!*
> *   I'd be for ever Thine;*
> *Confessing Thee, the living Word,*
> *My Saviour Christ, my God, my Lord,*
> *   Thy cross shall be my sign.*

7: *A New Companion: Charles Haddon Spurgeon*

To the best of my recollection it was the year 1930 when I first appreciated the value of the work of Charles Haddon Spurgeon, and the knowledge came through the reading of several of his sermons in the thick *Metropolitan Pulpit* volumes. In those days my personal library – and if I am to believe Victor Hugo, 'a library is an act of faith' – was somewhat scanty. It grew but slowly. The starting salary of a teacher even in a secondary or grammar school at that period was well under £6 a week. Before the famous Burnham scale of salaries came into operation the weekly salary of the headmaster himself of a secondary school of three or four hundred children was not more than £6. So that when rent had been paid (for few could afford to buy a house) and the needs of a growing family supplied, little was left for 'personal library' purposes.

It was a blessing to me that the price of second-hand books in those days was a mere fraction of today's prices. One could purchase old Puritan tomes, rich in spiritual nectar, for 'an old song'. Even ten or twelve years later I well remember the modernist school-colleague aforementioned asking me whether I was interested in purchasing two folio volumes (dated 1676) of Caryl on Job which one of his relations wished to dispose of without delay. They had been rebound with black leather spines and were in excellent condition, replete with a full-scale engraved portrait of the preacher. Joseph Caryl had been a member of the Westminster Assembly of Divines, and as his honoured name occasionally appeared in Strict Baptist publications I knew that he was worthy of a Christian's attention. Accordingly I visited the house indicated to me and discovered that the owner of the two volumes was chiefly interested in making more house room, and was only too glad to see Caryl leave the premises. The price asked for his commentary was five shillings. Did I buy it! I have not made as much use of it as I ought, I frankly confess, but it is one of the treats still in store – largely so – and I say 'largely' with a twofold meaning, for it is a stupendous work, the first volume having 2,282 columns of text (two columns to a page), the second 2,410, besides extensive end Tables. But the invaluable *Commenting and Commentaries* assures me that 'Caryl gives us much, but none too much. His work can scarcely be superseded or surpassed.' On an Edinburgh abridgement of 1836 (price 1*s* 6*d*) the further comment is passed, 'An ox in a gallipot is nothing to it'. It was refreshing to hear an Oxford postgraduate student (he hailed from Fifeshire), some years ago, explain to me how helpful he had found Caryl when he had been challenged to give the meaning of the verse, 'The noise thereof sheweth concerning it, the cattle also concerning the vapour' (*Job 36:33*).

Not long after purchasing Caryl I acquired from a North Wales bookseller a set of the Parker Society volumes, forty-nine in all, covering the entire range of English Reformation theology – Cranmer, Ridley, Latimer, Tyndale, Jewel, Hooper, and all! Their price was six pence ('old notation') per volume. Those were the days! But their very cheapness, and in Wales at that, illustrates the almost total lack of interest in historical theology, and in all biblical truth, too, alas! Certainly new religious books were being written and doubtless read, at least by a few, but the old theology was 'at a discount', and

[83]

the discount was prodigiously great. But my chapter is to concern Spurgeon, and to Spurgeon I turn.

I acquired my first volumes of the *Metropolitan Tabernacle Pulpit* in Manchester. In that somewhat grimy but loved city two or three second-hand bookshops adorned its Oxford Road, and in the doorway of one of them, attracting the eye of the passer-by, and not least mine, were shelves on which I found my never-to-be-forgotten treasure. I hardly suppose that their price was above a shilling a volume. Home they came, and before long I had tasted their sweet. To change the figure, it was not long before they gripped me like a magnet. There are sermons and sermons. Some go well into print, others appear pale and cadaverous. Some are fit but for the fire, others are like burnished gold. Spurgeon's, I found, belonged to the burnished class. I had so far come across nothing of their kind comparable to them. Philpot I knew, and Whitefield I knew, but these! I had sampled the cream of Scottish sermons in the three volumes of *The Free Church Pulpit: Sermons and Lectures by Eminent Scottish Divines* (published in 1852), and good they were, but these! They seemed nonpareil.

The Spurgeonic sermons, like Daniel's fourth beast, 'diverse from all the others' – readers will forgive the uncouth comparison – possessed outstanding characteristics. They were expository, and Bible-based; certainly not without application; doctrinal without being dry; practical without being excessively so; experimental without being sentimental or flabby. The more I read them the more I was impressed by their balance, by their freshness, by their apt illustrations of spiritual truth almost after the manner of Gurnall, indeed by their perfect 'technique', if such a term may be allowed me. I could supply illustrative examples without end, but must forbear to do so. At the same time I was captivated – I use the word deliberately –

by the sheer beauty of their language, by their sturdiness
of expression, by their charming diction. Like Dan
Chaucer, they seemed to be 'a well of English undefiled'.
No matter what the date of the volume into which I dipped
my bucket – for before long I had obtained many more
volumes than the Manchester three – the result was the
same. Whether 1862, 1882, or 1902, or whatever, their
quality remained unimpaired. It amazed me that sixty-
two volumes of sermons, throughout their entire range,
could maintain, on average, such a standard of excellence.
Here was pulpit genius indeed. I noted the difference, of
course, between sermons of the *New Park Street Pulpit*
volumes and those, say, of the 'eighties; again, between
sermons revised by the master-preacher himself (up to his
death in 1892) and the later twenty-five annual sermon
volumes which, though well edited, lacked 'the touch of a
vanished hand'. Yet 'the sound of a voice that was still'
remained. All in all, their quality was superb. I became a
Spurgeon lover, as too did my wife. We must have read at
least a thousand of the sermons aloud together.

Long after 1930 I came across the tribute paid by
Robertson Nicoll to Spurgeon. For certain reasons – and I
think they are well founded – I had learned not to value too
highly any commendation of a work from the pen of the
Editor of *The British Weekly*, but in this particular case I
was whole-heartedly with him. His tribute runs thus:

The influence of Spurgeon was not of those that have
passed, or that can pass away like a dream. Even yet,
people will explain his popularity by his voice, his
humour, by his oratory, and the like. But the continued
life and power of his printed sermons show that his
oratory, noble as it was, was not the first thing. Our firm
belief is that these sermons will continue to be studied
with growing interest and wonder; that they will
ultimately be accepted as incomparably the greatest

contribution to the literature of experimental Christianity that has been made in this century, and that their
message will go on transforming and quickening lives
after all other sermons of the period are forgotten
(Tribute printed at end of Sermon 2572, published in
1898).

I read sermons aloud to my wife so that we might enjoy
them simultaneously. In this way we derived increased
benefit. On reflection I see that there are three chief ways
of 'tasting' a sermon – the first, and doubtless the best, is
to hear it delivered by the living voice of its author; a
second is to read it in cold print; a third, and I would claim
that it is the second-best, is to read it, or to hear it read,
aloud. If the reader is sufficiently skilled, something of the
fervour and urgency of the preacher himself may be
recaptured. I discovered by the experiment that the
sermons had a penetrating quality which reached to heart
and mind and conscience. One such occasion I shall never
forget.

Three or four of my wife's relations – not parents or
sisters or brothers – happened to be with us in our home,
and I read to them. The sermon I selected – and I do not
think that I had read it previously – was on Amos 4:12:
'Prepare to meet thy God, O Israel' (No. 923, dated March
27, 1870). Spurgeon's preface – his prefaces are often
sermons in miniature in themselves, and strikingly
original – was followed by mention of the 'divers tones' in
which such words might be spoken, as for example to
Adam in paradise, to the believer engaged in private
devotions, to saints going up to the house of the Lord, to
believers meeting God in the disembodied state. From
such a delightful theme, cunningly worked out, the
sermon next moved to a consideration of 'Prepare to meet
thy God' as 'words of caution to the vast majority of men':
to the dying who know not the Lord, to the ungodly who

have set God's law at defiance. This concluded Part 1 of the sermon. Part 2 spoke the same five words as 'heavy tidings to the ungodly'. And here by means of italicized words and phrases the sinner was told about God's message 'for THEE, . . . for YOU, YOU, YOU must meet YOUR God . . . a God of *unblinded omniscience, infinite discernment, unsullied holiness, insulted mercy, everlasting truth, omnipotent power*' – six or eight lines of print on each phrase. Then came Part 3, entitled 'a weighty precept' – 'Prepare to meet thy God'. With all the skill of which he was such a pulpit-master, Spurgeon wrote his text, so to speak – and I tremble even now as I write the words – on his hearers' hearts, five or six thousand of them, listening doubtless as though the world was not, and as though eternity was nigh. They, they, they were to meet God! He warned them of their need of the Advocate, the Daysman, Jesus Christ the righteous, the one Saviour in the whole universe of being. He urged their own unrighteousness upon their inmost consciences to show them the peril in which they stood before the bar of infinite justice and the judgment throne of God. Finally, in what must have been a burst of surpassing eloquence of the most exalted kind, he spoke these words – gospel application at its tremendous best:

> Perhaps ere another Sabbath's bell shall ring, some of you now listening to my voice will be in the land of spirits and have passed the solemn test – weighed in the balances and found wanting. If it be so, and it were hard for any man here to prophesy that it shall not be so, for where several thousands are met together, the very chances of mortality, as men call them, go to make us fear it. The fact of this subject being thrust upon me, makes me feel as though a prophetic impulse were in it. Then, if it be so, you and I, whoever you may be, fated for death this week, stand in a peculiar relationship to each other.

I may be gazing straight into those eyes which shall never look upon me again till we meet at the judgment-bar, and if I be not faithful to your soul, you may rise up amidst that throng and say, 'I strayed into that Tabernacle, and I listened to you, but you played with your theme, you were not in earnest, and so I was lost.'

SO THEN I WILL BE IN EARNEST. I conjure thee by the living God, escape from the wrath to come! As the Lord liveth, there is but a step between thee and death! Flee for thy life! Look not behind thee! Turn thy whole soul to Jesus! A crucified Saviour waits for a lost sinner, willing to receive him, willing to receive him now!

Now thou canst not look me in the face in the next world, and say I did not speak to thee earnestly. O that the glance which we exchange at this moment may be succeeded in that tremendous day by a glance of recognition in which there shall be the soft emotions of gratitude and affection, as thou and I shall say to each other there, 'Blessed be God we met on that hallowed Sabbath-day, for now we shall meet for ever before the throne of him that liveth and was dead, and is alive for evermore, and hath the keys of hell and death.' God bless you, every one of you, richly, for Jesus' sake. Amen.

There is a reference in these words to the fact that on the Saturday evening before the morning on which the sermon was preached, Spurgeon was, as he says, sitting in his study 'about eight o'clock, revolving in my mind a subject for this hour's discourse' when 'there came a knock at my door and I was earnestly entreated by a father to hasten to the death-bed of his dear girl. I wanted much my time for preparation, but as the dear one was in such a case, and had long been a constant hearer of the word in this Tabernacle, I felt it my duty to go whether I could prepare a sermon or not . . . I see my sermons in sick rooms often, and I come to think of preaching sermons in a different light from what many do.'

My quotations are somewhat lengthy, but they are more than worthy of my present use. I read the sermon, or rather, most of it. Facing me as we sat together were, as I have explained, uncles and aunts of my wife, four of them, all elderly, and one only of them had confessed the name of the Lord in believer's baptism. Born and bred among Strict Baptists they had heard the Word times without number, but in the strict and biblical sense they yet remained outside the church of God. Lifelong attenders upon the means of grace, for one reason or another, they had not come to the point of confessing the Lord in any public way. Their lives were, to public view and to private knowledge, all that could be desired, upright, home-loving, generous, kind; and yet. . . ! My heart felt for them as I read the sermon. The words were indeed searching, and though I am not esteemed in any visible sense an emotional man, the moment came when I was too much charged with inward emotion to continue my reading. The final paragraphs had to be read by another. The room, the company, the occasion, the text, the discourse, are engraven upon the tablets of memory. Truth is masterful! truth is sublime! and thank God, truth is saving!

Week by week the sermon-reading continued. The discourses were nutritious, enlivening, soul-stirring, never dull. It is a temptation to quote paragraphs and sentences from them at length. But I must restrain my steeds as they champ at their bits, lest they carry me far off course.

My Scottish friends may be interested to know that Spurgeon was responsible for my first journey north of the Cheviots and even into 'Caledonia stern and wild'. I had been reading a sermon to my wife, but cannot now recall the text or even the nature of the discourse, but in the course of it Spurgeon remarked that he thought the canniness of the Scots was probably due, at least in part, to the fact that the Book of Proverbs played such a prominent part in their system of education, and doubtless in the instruction of their youth in church and home alike. Previously I had been disinclined to visit Scotland, for I am somewhat of a stay-at-home, a tribute to the high success of my wife's management, but the preacher's words caused me to say, 'Then we must go to see that wonderful country'. My wife kept me to my pledge! Happily, by that time we had a motor car, so could wander freely where we would, and very pleasant we found the trip to be. But I confess that I found the Edinburgh second-hand bookshops rather 'pricey', so did not do well in those quarters. Yet in other ways my library was growing steadily.

As explained earlier I had formed the practice of separating my duplicate sermon volumes into their component parts, fifty-two in number, so as to distribute sermons far and wide. Occasionally friends have told me by letter about blessings they have brought to them. As I write I recall the case of a friend resident in Cheshire to whom I sent a sermon (No. 1257–8) on the text, 'Jesus said unto them, If God were your Father, ye would love me'. The title of the discourse was 'Love to Jesus the Great Test'. He was enraptured with the sermon – I choose the word deliberately – took its message to heart, and although I must have sent it to him fifteen or twenty years ago (how speedily time flies!), last month I received from him this message: 'A Christian friend has typed me a copy of that wonderful sermon of Spurgeon which you so kindly sent me some time ago, and when I am well [he is an invalid] I will have some photostat copies made and send one to you.' Previously – he writes once a year – he had asked me for any other duplicate copies of the sermon that I might possess but I could not oblige him. At one time I could supply sermons to friends on a substantial range of texts. I think of an Anglican clergyman who pressed me hard in this way. But my hundred duplicate volumes became depleted and by now they have shrunk almost to nothing. I trust they have served the Lord's purpose. To my widowed step-mother, a Methodist, not much older than myself, I recall giving a sermon on the subject of the Lord's Supper. That, too, was maybe a dozen or more years ago, and I may claim that from that time she too became a Spurgeon lover. She read and re-read the sermon until, had it belonged to the world of the clothier, it would have been described as threadbare.

I freely confess that, after forty years and more, my early enthusiasm for the sermons has never waned. I do not read today anything like as many as formerly, but they remain my favourite reading in the sermonic department, and are as good to me as a square meal to the famished. If on a journey, especially by train, I usually carry one or two in my breast-pocket. I well remember once finding myself in London with an odd hour to occupy. Nearby was an Anglican Church with ever-open hospitality. I entered, found a seat, and with much profit and pleasure read a sermon on Judges 11:35: 'I have opened my mouth unto the Lord, and I cannot go back' (Vol. 23, No. 1341). It met my soul's need at that particular time, and was as a substantial meal. Indeed it seems to me that the Christian reader might well be encouraged to turn to the sermons in words that belong to the auctioneer's repertoire as he urges bargains upon his audience, 'You cannot go wrong'. I accept that some find the sermons so different from those to which they have long become accustomed to listen, that they have difficulty in getting an appetite for them. One or two have described them to me as 'flowery'. I do not consider the term justified, but I do accept that a man has a right to state his own reactions, and the enthusiast has to consider them. Possibly the late twentieth-century reader would find that to enjoy the sermons one needs nowadays something of an 'acquired taste'. The form in which they present divine truth is not that of many a pulpit of today, but it can never be said that their language is outdated except in such matters as 'thou' and 'thee'. Basically their language is true Anglo-Saxon refined by the Latin and other elements which in mediaeval times were grafted upon it. The thousands who hung upon Spurgeon's lips for thirty-six years did not complain of floweriness, obscurity, high-falutin propensities, or aught else. They listened to a servant of the Lord speaking out his heart and mind and soul in a language which they could well understand, from the costermonger of the streets to the aristocrats of the highest circles in the land. And to the ends of the earth the printed discourses were blown to the nations like thistle-down, not to sow the earth with noxious growth, but to spread the wisdom from above, and the 'fruit of righteousness which is sown in peace of them that make peace'. 'Dinna forget Spurgeon' was the parting cry of the wife of the Scottish highlander as her husband went to market; and to the weekly pamphlet brought home from the stall many owed, under God, their soul's nutriment.

I recall only one now distant occasion when a sermon was abused, and I must be blamed to the extent of being the sermon's donor. A young man of my acquaintance, a novice in the ministry of the Word, had been invited to 'take a service'. He had consented. His sermon, which I heard, sounded suspiciously unlike what one would have expected to be his normal manner of speech, for after all, a man in the pulpit is not expected to speak in a language entirely at variance with his everyday utterance. I was set a-wondering. Ere long I realised what was happening. He was repeating the sermon of Spurgeon as though it were his own, or at least, a substantial part of it. To make the mention of the incident complete I must add that the young man, though not by any means unintelligent, in this case bewrayed himself. He went on unthinkingly until he made reference to a happening in the United States – it was either in Colorado or California – which must have been dated about 1865 or 1870, but the foolish young fellow gave it as though it were an event of his own day and time. If he has long forgotten the discrepancy, I have not, but I never charged him with the fault, for I had not invited him to 'take the service'.

One domestic incident I must mention. It arose through the reading of the sermons with my wife. It dates from December 1931. We already had one son and a second was expected. The latter received his name sermon-wise. The particular sermon in this case was about one of the Johns of the New Testament, whether the Baptist or the Apostle I do not remember. My wife had earlier expressed the desire that, if the second child proved to be a boy, he should be named John. Apparently I had different thoughts, though after this long lapse of time I fail to remember where my own choice lay. But the sermon gave me a change of mind. John was the sermon's theme, John therefore was in my thoughts, and ere I finished the reading, or it may have been a few minutes afterwards, I was led to say, 'I agree, if it is a boy, his name must be John'. And John it was!

Another writer of worth plays a small part in connection with the birth of our first child. The date was 1928. I lived five miles from the school where I was a teacher, and to cover the distance, including a long uphill climb on returning home, I bought a motor cycle. It possessed a belt-drive, which slipped around its two wheels helplessly in wet weather, and brought the machine to a standstill; but that has no bearing on my story. The day came when I decided to dispose of the cycle and to return to the push-cycle of former use, so I motored over to the Wirral peninsula in the hope of finding a purchaser. My quest met with no success. But during the return journey I somewhere came across a two-volume copy of John Brown's *Commentary on the First Epistle of Peter* (1849). It still bears its price-mark: 'Two shillings'; yet the volumes are substantial. I had no carrier on my cycle so I tucked the two volumes into the folds of my mackintosh. Some twenty miles from home I was discovered lying unconscious on the road alongside my motor cycle. What caused the mishap I never knew; no other vehicle was involved and I had never been known to faint. I surmise that my tyres slipped on sun-heated tar, for 'summer was nigh'. The impact took from me all memory of the cause, if I ever really knew it.

I returned to consciousness to find myself in a farmhouse in the care of a kind couple named Williams – a good Welsh name! The precious volumes were there also, the spine of one of them bearing, as it still does, the plain evidence of contact with black tar. I was fearfully sick and it was thought that I had fractured my skull. Shortly, a kindly doctor from my own village came and took me home in his car. The motor cycle followed me later, but was never again used by me, perhaps wisely so! The accident, and the nervous shock that it gave to my wife, led to the birth of our first-born, a month prematurely. Maybe his name should have been Peter, to remind me of the accident, but we had already agreed upon 'David', and David it remained.

I mention the happening partly to explain that it has supplied me with confirmation in a certain matter, namely, the assurance of salvation. I distinctly remember that, in semi-consciousness after my fall, the first words I spoke to the farmer and his wife concerned the truth of God. I found myself telling them that I believed with all my heart in the words, 'By grace are ye saved through faith; and that not of yourselves: it is the gift of God: not of works lest any man should boast' (*Eph. 2:8–9*). What they thought of my words I could not guess, but to me at least they have been a source of comfort as I reflect on the fact that the truth of God's grace – and that to me! – was firmly fixed in my subconscious mind, and that such an event brought it to the light of day. 'O God, my heart is fixed, my heart is fixed; I will sing and give praise' (*Psalm 57:7; 108:1*).

One word more about Spurgeon. I came to value all his books, though none of them occupied the same place in my heart as did the sermons. His *Treasury of David* is my favourite reading on the Psalms. Spurgeon's own comments followed by the quotations which he appends from a vast variety of authors I have invariably found good and useful. Then, too, all the volumes of *The Sword and the Trowel*, the monthly magazine which Spurgeon launched in 1866, furnish excellent reading. They furnish sermons not found in the *Metropolitan Tabernacle Pulpit* volumes, and articles of biographical, historical and theological value. Their book reviews, mostly from the Editor's own pen, are pungent, sometimes amusing, and never dull. One review in particular I call to mind; I imagine it to be unique of its kind. The reviewer found himself reading a certain book favourably, but ere long he found disagreeable Romish tendencies, which he terms 'the smell of Roman candles'. As he read on he encountered more such noxious odours, and in sheer revolt he flung the book into the corner of the room. Later, relenting, he went to recover it, found its back broken, and picked it up muttering 'served it right'. There the review ended!

Spurgeon's four-volume autobiographical volumes were sheer delight, particularly the first pair of volumes. Much improved in presentation, trimmed and suitably augmented, they add their substantial quota to the list of books published by the Banner of Truth Trust, and supply much information about their subject not to be found elsewhere. The re-publication of the *Metropolitan Tabernacle Pulpit* volumes both in America and Britain is a notable event in the realm of truth. God speed the sale! Now that the feast is spread, may many hearken to the call!

I cannot but commend that which I find to be good, and I cannot but rejoice in a ministerial career which has meant, and still means, so much to me. When I reflect on Spurgeon's career, his humble beginnings, his lack of a university education, his impact on the nation and the church of God, his magnificent contribution to the interests of the kingdom of God, I am compelled to say, 'Here was a Caesar; when comes there such another!' And one word I would add for the encouragement of any obscure mother or other person who may be entrusted by God with the so-important work of rearing children. Spurgeon was never ashamed to confess that he had learned not a little of his theology from 'the old cook', Mary King, a person who, when a sermon was of little worth, warmed her theological faculties in the same way as did a hen scratching over a heap of rubbish. 'I do believe', says the Autobiography, 'that I learnt more from her than I should have learned from any six doctors of divinity of the sort we have nowadays. The cook at Newmarket was a godly experienced woman, from whom I learned far more than I did from the minister of the chapel we attended.' Doubtless had the power to confer D.Ds. been Spurgeon's she would have received one, for, said he, 'so many D.Ds. are fiddle-de-dees'. But I close on a biblical note befitting the theme: 'Unto you which believe, there is honour' (*1 Pet. 2:7*).

8: *Treasure Hunts around Wales and Beyond*

I have previously explained that Reformation, Puritan and later works of evangelical value were 'at a discount' in the period of my conversion and for some years afterwards, but that my book collection grew somewhat slowly for financial reasons. As times and circumstances improved, however, I made progress, and was able to take better advantage of the situation in the second-hand bookshops. Manchester, Chester, Liverpool and sundry other towns had such shops, the first-named having also a kind of open-air book mart situated in Shudehill where also its hen market was to be found. Further west there were two such shops known to me in Caernarvonshire and another at Wrexham in Denbighshire. Shrewsbury, though not of course in Wales, also had its two or three booksellers. Otherwise I knew of no other possible sources of 'treasures' in North Wales. In South Wales, Carmarthen, Swansea, Cardiff, and not least Aberystwyth, had shops that came to my knowledge, some better, some poorer.

But it was approaching 1940 before I was able to make much progress in this activity. By that time I had a car of sorts, but severe petrol rationing during the period of the Second World War brought severe problems in its wake. I remember that one was able to buy only about two gallons per week, and certainly, in the most literal sense, that did not go very far. When the situation eased off somewhat as the war came to an end, I was able to take journeys further afield, and to add Oswestry, London, Bristol, Bath, Southampton, and even Norwich on one occasion to my questing list.

I had several reasons for wishing to acquire certain types of books. Professionally, History, my subject of study, demanded quite wide reading if I was to keep in touch with the subject in anything like its fullness. To teaching I added the work of marking some five hundred 'O' level History scripts a year for one of England's examining boards – an assignment and a toil which I have continued for the past thirty years. I found that it greatly added to one's efficiency as a teacher of the subject, kept one to a national standard (and to a scale of standards) of achievement, and brought one into touch each year with the work of a considerable variety of schools scattered over a wide area. No mean benefits! This work, too, also required one to keep *au fait* with historical writing. Additionally I had taken responsibility for Scripture teaching in the school where I served, both at 'O' and 'A' levels, the Advanced work in particular necessitating constant resort to commentaries and suchlike works. At the same time I remained school librarian with about £100 per year available for purchases of books new and old. So all in all I had good cause to keep in touch with the book market both new and second-hand. Thus far my apologia for being a book lover, a book reader, and a book hunter! If I am anything further I hold the Banner of Truth Trust responsible! But I must here confine myself to books of Christian worth and importance.

I speak chiefly of Wales because of my long contact with it both geographically and culturally, and to some extent spiritually. Its hills and its valleys, its history past and present, its people and its chapels, its ministers and its aspirations, I learned at first hand. Speaking generally, I would judge that the spiritual decline set in well before the close of the nineteenth century. The Higher Critics, gathering strength say from 1880 onwards, made great inroads; the Evan Roberts revival of 1904 seemed to do little to stem the decline of sound doctrine, especially in the six northern counties of Wales. So that by the time I began to reside in Wales the spiritual dearth seemed to me to be alarmingly great. The *Old Memories* of Sir Henry Jones, a native of Llangerniew in Denbighshire – later he became Professor of Moral Philosophy in the University of Glasgow – had recorded that in the religious revival of 1859, when Henry Jones was a lad of seven, 'the evidence of the presence and power of the "Spirit" was overwhelming':

> Men and women were quite genuinely beside themselves with religious excitement. They broke out in the services, glorifying God by the help of hymns and verses, and not infrequently in language . . . marvellous in its power and beauty . . . I watched the finest of the church elders, one of the ablest men I have ever met, go from end to end of the chapel and up and down its aisles, on his knees praising God all the time and manifestly in the power of an overwhelming force.

The life of the Calvinistic Methodists of the village became intense. In addition to Sunday services, they met on Monday for the prayer-meeting; on Tuesday came the children's catechising meeting; on Wednesday evening the singing meeting; on Thursday the church meeting in which the older folk shared their religious experiences of the week; and on Friday evening was the young men's meeting. In Llangerniew they had no minister; the chapel elders took full control. The Evan Roberts revival was doubtless somewhat similar in its results.

But little, if any, of this spiritual fervour remained by 1920 or 1930. I received the distinct impression that fervent, old-fashioned spiritual exercise and experience was a thing of the past; even of the remote past. It seemed almost, if not quite, as dead as the dodo. The generation of ministers which corresponded to the former state of religion had gone too, with very rare exceptions. I knew but one in my own locality. Their libraries had come into the second-hand market and had already been dispersed or perhaps in some cases destroyed. A few, a very few, remained and were awaiting the by no means tender treatment of a new and in certain ways 'an untoward generation', which had little respect for the beliefs of its forbears. World War I had almost been a watershed between ancient and modern, spiritual and secular. 'New thought' had replaced 'the old ways'. College and especially university education had brought new forces to bear on the undergraduate race. The old faith was virtually fighting for its life. I say again that the second-hand book market reflected this situation. I give a concrete illustration of what may denote a widespread epidemic.

A school colleague of mine (who had once amazed me by asking me to lend him a commentary to help him compose a discourse on 'Because thou art neither cold nor hot I will spew thee out of my mouth') once told me that the widow of a deceased elderly (Welsh Presbyterian) minister had a few of her late husband's books to dispose of, and he suggested that they might have an interest for me. I thought so too, so without much delay I visited the lady and found she had a bare dozen or score volumes. Their small number surprised me so I inquired what had happened to the rest of her husband's books. She informed me that they remained with her son who lived some ten or twelve miles away. I went over to see him, and was grieved to find that he had cleared a bookcase of all the ministerial books and consigned them to the floor of a leaking cinder-shed. Any that I cared to retrieve, he told me, I was welcome to take away. When I inspected them I found that some were already suffering badly from damp and dirt and neglect; in fact several were already rotting away and I could do nothing with them. But among the rest were a fair number I was glad to acquire, including almost forty volumes of Calvin's works (Calvin Translation Society edition), several volumes of the Nichol series of Puritan works, and other books of worth. I inquired the price and was told that I could have them *gratis* if I would but take them away. I gave a reward to his small daughter, and feeling somewhat sad at heart to see such volumes treated so contemptuously, I took my departure with the treasure. It did not comfort my heart to learn that the generous donor was himself a schoolmaster.

On another occasion the small personal library of a local Roman Catholic priest came under the hammer, and I acquired a part of it. It contained some Protestant volumes of worth which later proved useful to me. I am not quite certain about the following, but I seem to remember that I obtained a copy of the famed Pastor Chiniquy volume in this way. I certainly obtained my first copy of the Latin Vulgate at the sale. It was a good leather-bound copy, which I should surmise had been very little used, and it contained an inscription stating that it had been presented to its first owner when, in Rome, in 1914, he was ordained to the priesthood.

A well-known Welsh bookseller, and at the same time a local preacher near and far, lived at Caernarvon. He was approaching old age when first I made contact with him. His shop, small and congested, was under the shadow of the great Edwardian castle where in recent days the present Prince of Wales was invested as Prince at the hands of the Queen his mother. Occasionally, if he found that in his second-hand department trade was dull, he would offer books at bargain prices, and I once acquired from him almost the whole of the twelve-volume *Oxford*

Dictionary of massive proportions. It took forty years to compile (1888–1928) and gives what is virtually a complete history of all words in the English language, together with illustrative quotations drawn from all periods. A most interesting work! The first three volumes which thus came to me were cloth-bound (each one weighs approximately twelve pounds), the rest was in the original parts, but unhappily one small section was missing. It has been a most useful possession.

About half a mile from the castle and shop in Caernarvon, alongside the River Seiont, was an old schoolhouse, large and empty. My bookseller had obtained the use of it, I imagine by purchase, shelved it, and filled it with libraries small and large that he had acquired. He allowed favoured customers to visit it, and explore its contents at their leisure. I should add that this was not so easy an operation as it might sound, for the shelves were not at all easy of access, especially in their upper reaches. Some were high and the titles of books almost out of the range of vision. The difficulty of access arose from the fact that, when the shelves had been filled, later acquisitions were dumped on the floor which, in time, came to be covered by a mountain of volumes in great confusion, and one had literally to burrow into the mass to get any idea as to its contents. Sets of works might be scattered into corners, and it was a great labour to join 'bone to his bone'. After a time the old bookseller disposed of his business to a younger man who appeared to lack interest in the second-hand book trade, and who was only too glad to allow such a person as myself to visit the schoolhouse (what better place for a schoolmaster?), load up the car, return to the shop, strike a bargain (about £5 per load) and depart. In this way I obtained some very serviceable volumes. About three years ago when I paid the new proprietor a courtesy call (for I suspected that the old schoolhouse stock was no more), he informed me with sorrow that boys had broken into the schoolhouse and done so much damage to it, even to the pulling down of the shelves. He had therefore sent all the stock that remained to a pulping factory.

A Colwyn Bay emporium, long closed down – most second-hand bookshops in Wales ultimately close down, for time brings its changes – also proved useful to me. One particular treasure which I found there was a copy of the Bagster *Biblia Sacra Polyglotta* (edited by Samuel Lee); in other words a magnificent gilt-edged folio-size leather-bound work, showing on its double page, eight versions of the Scriptures. As I write it lies open before me at the Book of Psalms, and gives the Hebrew, the Greek Septuagint, the English Authorised Version, and the Latin on the one page; and German, French, Italian and Spanish translations on the other page. In the New Testament section the only change is that the Septuagint gives way to the original Greek of the text, and the Hebrew is a translation of the Greek text also. In the same store I acquired, in addition, a Polyglot Bible of German origin (six volumes) and a Hexaglot of another type. 'The time would fail me' to tell of other similar works that I 'picked up' here and there.

Bangor was another of my hunting grounds, its market place and its bookshops, not to mention a private house as well. Looking back I realise how incredibly low were its prices, even though a university college and one or two denominational colleges were 'nigh at hand'. And even no price at all on occasion! I had been a good customer in the chief of the bookshops. One day when it seemed that the proprietor himself despaired of finding fresh 'old' stock, I found piled high on the floor about sixty half-yearly volumes of *The Christian World Pulpit*. I hasten to say that this series was not by any means uniformly good. The sermons were by all kinds of preachers, denominationally and theologically, but in my opinion they are very useful as indicating the character of the late Victorian and Edwardian pulpit from approximately 1880 to 1910. Some of the sermons are of first-rate evangelical quality, but others are of a very different calibre. But the amazing thing was that the proprietor of the bookshop told me that I could take the sixty volumes free of charge if I would only take them off his hands! He preferred their room to their company. Close by, in a tiny bookroom behind a small stationer's shop I remember acquiring ten volumes of State Trials, folio, complete from the earliest recorded times to about 1760: price one guinea! They were a bookseller's lumber in those not very distant days!

I have still to mention another free gift of books that came to me. The scene accordingly moves to the cathedral city of St Asaph. I was informed one day by a friendly town librarian with whom I kept in touch, that he had been offered by a local councillor a 'crazy pile' of old books which lay on the floor of a garage at St Asaph, some distance from his own library. After inspecting it he had come to the conclusion that, with a few exceptions, the pile contained nothing that was at all suitable for public use, nor did the remaining volumes appeal in any way to his personal tastes. I was therefore free to take my fill, if only I would remove the unsightly heap from the spot where it lay. I fulfilled the conditions and discovered some quite useful volumes among the castaways. To my surprise they were throw-outs from the Cathedral Library, but how they came to meet with such an ignominious fate I never knew.

The best volume was an old small folio of 1646, supplying the original charges – and very detailed they were – against Archbishop William Laud, the arch-persecutor of the Puritans, who had been executed under Parliament's 'ordinance of attainder' in January, 1645.

The book was virtually the indictment against him, and had been compiled by William Prynne whom Laud (acting through the revived Court of Star Chamber) had branded on the cheeks, deprived of his ears (or what remained of them, for there had been a previous shearing), fined £5,000, and sentenced to life imprisonment. The branding was with the letters 'S.L.' (Seditious Libeller), but, redoubtable lawyer that he was, Prynne interpreted them as *Stigmata Laudis*. For a time he had been imprisoned in Caernarvon Castle in order to isolate him from his friends (and it must be remembered that parts of Wales were in those times some ten days' journey from London). Some other volumes in the pile were also of interest to me.

Possibly in many personal libraries the principal contents carry personal reminiscences. It is so with mine. Some books one would hardly like to part with for a king's ransom. Others, like despisers of the Lord, are 'but lightly esteemed'. What surprises me is that, on occasions, the weight of the treasures I carried home (as though by galleon from the Indies) did not strain the springs of my cars (for one replaced another as time passed) to breaking point. The only time I suffered a trouble at all like to this was in Scotland when returning from a holiday in the Western Highlands, and a half-shaft broke. But books were 'not guilty'. I had carried an excessive passenger load over some shockingly bad roads in the Ben Nevis area. But I was passing through Paisley when the blow actually fell, and took my party homewards by train.

A further Bangor windfall deserves mention. Not that it gave me many books of importance, but it illustrates how winds blow from a variety of quarters. A minister named Thomas Shankland, a Baptist and a scholar of some repute – he was an expert, for example, in all matters linked with Thomas Charles of Bala – had become custodian of the

University College Welsh Library, Bangor. He died, and
a school colleague – how helpful they can be! – who lived
in Bangor told me that the surviving daughter of Mr
Shankland had her father's personal library to dispose of.
So I called to see her. As I expected, many of the books
were in 'a language that I understood not', and regretfully
I lacked the capacity to lay hold of it, though its
acquisition would certainly have been useful to me as a
teacher of much Welsh history. But there were other
volumes of theological worth which I was glad to obtain,
all identifiable later by the pencilled initials 'T.S.' I
thought I had acquired *The Morning Star, or, Divine Poems
of Mr Rees Prichard, sometime Vicar of Llandovery,
Carmarthenshire* (London, 1785) from this source; but as I
look at it again I find that it was a Caernarvon acquisition.
The work is a very useful English translation of evangelical verses in abundance, first published in Wales in the
mid-seventeenth century under the title of *The Welshman's
Candle*. They were very popular indeed in the land of the
Cymry.

Aberystwyth, I found, was well worth a visit. I arrived
opportunely on one occasion, for the old manager of the
town's chief bookshop had just retired and a younger man
had stepped into his place. The shop contained a small
department which the old manager, for some reason
unknown to me, had sealed off from the public. The new
manager had just opened it up when I arrived. I cannot
claim that the treasures it contained were comparable to
those of the famed tomb of an ancient Pharaoh, but they
were such as caused me some little amazement. And what
was more, the price for a purchase in any quantity was six
pence, and certainly not more than a shilling, a copy. A
shop-window set of books which I bought at a later date in
the same shop enhanced the interest and value of my
collection of missionary books. They are *The Matabele*

Journals of Robert Moffat (1829–60), pioneer missionary in South Africa and father-in-law of David Livingstone who married his daughter Mary in 1844. The *Journals* had long been lost sight of, until in 1941 they were discovered in an iron-bound pine chest at Quagga's Kerk in Cape Province. Obviously their discovery renders all previous Lives of Moffat out of date. I was glad to obtain them, as for certain reasons I had a special interest in the man. I once possessed an autograph letter of his, dated 1879, but to my later regret I parted with it. But I am happy to own one of the original Baxter prints showing Moffat at the age of forty-three. He, like Livingstone, was one of whom the world was not worthy.

In Liverpool I once acquired Thomas Milner's *Life of Isaac Watts*, superseded now to some extent by later Lives of the poet but valuable in its day (1834). Its value was vastly enhanced by reason of the fact that it contained, as inserts made by a former owner, two long holograph letters of Watts and a quantity of his sermon notes, written in a form of shorthand, but with a few words in longhand to guide the preacher's eye as he used the notes in the pulpit. The better of the two letters, dated 1717, relates some of his experiences in that year when he was laid aside from his London congregation by illness. It is a pastoral letter and includes the words:

> If there be any secret sin for which God yet contends with me, I long to have it discovered that there might be no more cause of further contention betwixt my God and me. O may the good spirit of prayer be with you that at length ye may prevail, and lay a foundation for much thanksgiving . . . I long to serve Him, and I think I value my life for no other purpose. But He wants me not, nor my poor services, and however He deals with me, I join heartily with all your prayers for the spiritual and eternal welfare of this Church, to which I am

engaged in all the bonds of love, gratitude and the Gospel.

Your unworthy and afflicted brother and servant,

I. Watts

Written at Theobalds
Feb. 12:1717/8.

At Aylesbury in Buckinghamshire I once obtained two holograph letters written by James Montgomery, the hymn-writer, of Sheffield. One of them is a reply to an invitation to be present at a wedding; it is dated 1839. It includes the words, so unexpected in the case of one who wrote hymns of such great assurance:

> I have been from home the greater part of the last three months and unwell all the time. From whatever cause, I have suffered so much from mental depression that I have spirit for no undertaking beyond daily occupations – and even these are very indifferently performed – so that I am compelled to decline every engagement which comes not upon me as an absolute obligation.

Apparently the invitation had playfully remarked upon Montgomery's failure to marry, and on this point he remarked:

> You know by personal experience that the loss and the misfortune are my own; whether the fault be so I must leave others to judge in charity, where there is no evidence. The secret is with myself and it is on the way to the grave, from which no secret will be betrayed till the day of judgment.

Montgomery, born at Irvine in Ayrshire, was sixty-seven at the time of his writing the letter. He lived fifteen years longer. His hymns are a choice legacy to the church of God.

In a place of which I have no recollection I obtained a holograph letter sent by Spurgeon to the pastor of a Baptist church in Glasgow. More valued still by me is the sheet of his sermon notes when he preached from John 8:56 ('Your father Abraham rejoiced to see my day, and he saw it and was glad'). The discourse is No. 2652 in the 1899 volume of the *Metropolitan Tabernacle Pulpit*, but actually it was preached in July, 1882. The notes fill one side of a small piece of letter paper (black edged) which must have reached Spurgeon to intimate a death. On the reverse side the sheet shows the numbers of the three hymns sung during the service.

I may add that I received this much-valued bit of paper as a gift from a member of the Open Air Mission (London) who told me that such sheets were being sold for a shilling at the time he bought it. That was certainly 'in the days of long ago'. Mrs Spurgeon frequently presented copies of her husband's books to preachers, and with the gift there was usually a slip written in her own hand. I possess two such slips, and they lie cheek by jowl in my little collection of holographs, as it were in fitting embrace. Mrs Spurgeon's Book Fund was a source of blessing to many. In her benefactions she shared her husband's world-wide ministry.

I forbear to give details of old Puritan folios and smaller volumes that have come my way, as to do so would overstretch my chapter. There is a distinct pleasure in handling them occasionally, even if, as in the case, say, of John Owen, Thomas Goodwin and Richard Sibbes, their works can be consulted and read in much more readable editions; for example, the Nichol series, or the Goold edition of Owen. The Nichol series was splendidly edited by A. B. Grosart for the most part. The lesser-known Puritan commentaries in the same series – larger volumes than the collected works – were also within reach of the purchaser (at second-hand) in those halcyon days. Thomas Adams on 2 Peter, and William Greenhill on Ezekiel are among them.

Biographies by the dozen came into my willing lap. Thirty-six leather-bound annual volumes of Spurgeon's *The Sword and the Trowel*, I obtained in Manchester. A duplicate set I later passed on to Mr Iain Murray. Commentaries by Keil, Delitzsch, Hengstenberg, Godet, and similar men were not too difficult to obtain. One had only to let down one's net, as it were, to enclose a multitude of fish.

In Shrewsbury I met with varied experiences. An antique shop once offered me a typical album of Victorian days (compiled about 1865). Its compiler, it appeared, had written to all kinds of nineteenth-century celebrities seeking their autographs. I should judge that he had been very successful, for in his album were signatures by the score of statesmen, writers, preachers, and others. In a few cases there were full-scale letters also. Dickens, J. H. Newman, Disraeli figured among them. Franked envelopes abounded from the days before penny postage. In this way I came into the possession of the signatures of such men as David Livingstone, H. M. Stanley, C. H. Spurgeon (an addition to the rest), James Montgomery (four lines of verse), S. S. Wesley (the musician, grandson of Charles Wesley), George Müller, S. P. Tregelles, and very many more.

My other chief Shrewsbury experience was somewhat different. In its market hall I fell for a beautifully-bound set (six large quarto volumes) of Adam Smith's *Commentary on the Bible*; with Spurgeon I agree that it is far from being the best of its kind, but it has its uses, and in the binding of my set it most certainly adorns a bookshelf. But I had to pay for it twice over, for as I returned with my package to my car, a vigilant limb of the law awaited me and charged me with overstaying my time in a parking area. In due course I had to pay the penalty of my fault. I rewarded the constable for his vigilance with a copy of a Scripture booklet entitled 'The Good Shepherd'. He seemed more than a little surprised. But he went on to perform his duty, and left me reflecting on one of the dangers of entering a bookshop!

I left Norwich one summer's day with a copy of Samuel Johnson's two-volume *Dictionary of the English Language* (second edition, 1756), quite a literary treasure. Its value in my eyes was doubled by the presence on each title page of the signature of Charles Simeon. Later I decided to sell the two volumes, but not before scissors had snipped off the valued memento of one of England's greatest evangelicals. My heart smote me afterwards, as did David's heart when he cut off a piece of Saul's robe, remembering that the king was 'the Lord's anointed'. All of sound judgment will agree that in a far higher sense the Cambridge preacher was the anointed of the Lord, and I began to feel that I was not honouring his memory by cutting off his name from a pair of books that he must often have consulted. Perhaps I should not have parted with the books, but, after all, house space has its limitations, and the pocket, too, has an end to its depth.

A schoolmaster of the present day would have much difficulty, I fear, in acquiring the type and variety of volumes that I obtained so readily. But since 'new times demand new measures' as well as 'new men', and 'God fulfils himself in many ways', there must be ways and means of overcoming difficulties which were not present in what I can only term 'my day'. 'Sufficient unto the day is the evil thereof.' And by young persons who fail to rise to a university education, it should be remembered – and I quote the words of a well-known university professor of English – that 'to many a poor man the English Bible has been a University'. I once heard a trainee-teacher holding forth to a class. He was in something of a flurry, for his college supervisor was also present, and inadvertently he asked the class to turn to 'The Book of the King of kings'! I trust that the supervisor did not lay such a fault to his charge.

9: *A Circle of Friends*

The informal house-meetings to which I made reference in an earlier chapter soon gave place to the more usual type of meetings for worship conducted publicly, and in 1935, on account of certain providential changes that intervened – and time inevitably brings its changes – it became necessary for me virtually to take pastoral charge of the fellowship. I continued to do so for eleven years.

It was in these years, following upon the period of Hitler's rule in Germany, and the failure of England's 'policy of appeasement', that the nations again fell into conflict.

In spiritual things it had a considerable impact upon us, living in North Wales, and that in two distinct ways. In the first place, large military camps appeared in the area, and it was not long before military personnel, commissioned and non-commissioned, put in an appearance at our meetings. It was a delight to meet them. Their presence recalled my own army days to mind and the help that I had received both from civilians and from fellow-conscripts. It had been a matter of shame to me that the farmer-friend who had most befriended me in days of military training and who, of course, passed out of sight when training ended, could not be recognised by me when, unexpected and unannounced, he called to see me in my home some twenty or twenty-five years later. Maybe time had brought about some change of countenance, but I never forgave myself my failure.

Our new soldier friends belonged to all shades of the evangelical spectrum – Pentecostals, Methodists, Baptists, Open Brethren, Presbyterians, Congregationalists, and a sprinkling of Anglicans. Some were Calvinistic, others Arminian; some hardly knew the spiritual difference between their right hand and their left. Hospitality was a problem but my wife rose splendidly to the occasion, or rather, to the occasions, for they were many, despite an arthritic affliction which told increasingly upon her as the years went by. We had very happy fellowship with some of our visitors, and a few of them remained in contact with us by letter or by an occasional visit for long years to come.

One such visit comes to mind. It was made by a friend who later became a schoolmaster. It was a visit during which he noted a change in our home which, to him, was decidedly regrettable. During the days of his 'military' calls upon us, we had on the dining-room walls certain portraits of evangelical worthies, the principal frame including portraits of Charles Wesley (whose hymns raised him well above his better-known brother in my personal opinion) and George Whitefield, discreetly kept apart by Selina, Countess of Huntingdon. John Foxe, too, and others were to be seen. We described them to our visitors as 'our relations'. As years went by the portraits became somewhat discoloured, by reason of the fact that my own picture-framing work was too amateurish to be good (I have learned since that the exclusion of dust and damp is a primary essential). So when our friend reappeared after a long interval of time the walls lacked their former glory. It was his nature to express his feelings openly and freely, and he was not slow to express his keen disappointment. But he was relieved to find that the 'good old doctrine' remained in all its beauty and integrity!

During the war period, we had occasional fellowship with Mr and Mrs Herman Newmark, Mr Newmark being Director of the Hebrew Christian Testimony to Israel. Mr B. S. Fidler, founder of the Barry Bible College, South Wales, who had once been a schoolmaster in Flintshire and who, though an Englishman, mastered the Welsh tongue, once visited us and gave us a helpful address upon the Epistle to Philemon. Dr John Wilmot, pastor of Highgate Road Chapel where he was the successor of James Stephens, was also a welcome visitor. Somewhat later in time came Dr Ernest F. Kevan, Principal of the London Bible College, who was ministering the Word from the Epistle of James at meetings of the China Inland Mission held in the neighbourhood. He was anxious to comb my library to find out whether I was in possession of any old Puritan volumes – not so much folios as books of smaller proportions – which might further his studies. He was engaged in the preparation of the thesis on 'The Grace of Law' which brought him his doctorate at the University of London. My library was able to render him some little assistance. As he left he gave me a list of Puritan authors, and impressed upon me his eager desire to obtain my further help in their acquisition.

Annually Dr Martyn Lloyd-Jones paid a visit, not to us, except on one remembered occasion, but to the area, and preached a sermon either in the largest building in the town or in the largest chapel, which happened to be the Welsh Presbyterian Chapel. I still recall the eagerly-awaited occasions when the entire countryside seemed to flock together, and to hang upon the lips of the preacher. Should these lines ever come to the notice of 'the Doctor', he will find me confessing to my shame that I have difficulty in remembering the themes of his discourses that my own ears heard, but less difficulty in remembering the themes of discourses which my wife or other relations or friends heard, I myself being unable to be present. I am somewhat perplexed by this and cannot account for the difference. The themes of sermons heard by others come fairly readily to mind after a long period of time. One was the death of John the Baptist and to this day my wife remembers the vivid reality of the tragedy as it was presented to view by the Doctor's word, and doubtless too by the use of his hands, for hands play a large part in the context of eloquence. Another discourse, by dint of context less vivid in its presentation, was based on Romans 10:3, where Paul deals with the problem of the unbelieving Jews' attempt to justify themselves by works. A third remembered sermon took the hearers to Daniel chapter 2, and appears to have concentrated upon the falling of the stone upon the feet of the image seen by Nebuchadnezzar. My friend who gave me the information was disappointed that 'the Doctor' referred the stone's falling to the first advent of Christ and not to his second advent. Still another sermon heard by others was that based on Ephesians 2:10: the Christian as God's workmanship, his *poiema*, his work of art. My father-in-law who was present long referred to the preacher's hands as they moved up and down in imitation of the work of a potter shaping his vessel according to the shape in which it seemed good to the potter to make it. I expect that Jeremiah's wonderful eighteenth chapter was quoted. My aged relation would demonstrate the shaping with his own hands – he had been a skilled craftsman himself, in carpentry, in his day – and went on to assure us that ere the preacher completed this part of his discourse, he, the hearer, had, in his mind's eye, actually seen the artist's workmanship complete – 'a vessel as seemed good to the potter to make it'. Knowing well, as I did, Dr Lloyd-Jones' style of approach to Paul's Epistles, I could well reach conclusions as to the content of this particular sermon.

I cudgel my memory almost in vain, but it tells me that I heard Dr Lloyd-Jones speak in North Wales on 'Christians as the Epistles of Christ', a sermon based on 2 Corinthians 3:3. It was good to be reminded of the Spirit of the living God writing his law on the fleshy tables of human hearts. And I recall that there was considerable emphasis on the characteristics of a letter.

I am in the predicament of having no diary to which to turn for records of the past, the only diary that I ever kept having reference to the period 1920 to 1924. But who knows that, when he is 'come to years', a publishing house will ask him for his reminiscences? And when such a request is made, who dares to refuse? While being very far indeed from having attained the years of a Jacob, there is an inclination of heart to say, as he said, 'The days of the years of my pilgrimage are . . . few and evil have the days of the years of my life been, and have not attained unto the days of the years of the life of my fathers in the days of their pilgrimage' (*Gen. 47:9*). Yet our years are numbered according to the wisdom of the Highest. Some I have known who were called home in their prime, others who have longed for the home-call which has seemed to them so long delayed.

It has not often been my lot to hear speakers whose names are household words among the children of God. One has normally to live in or near great cities to share such joys. For the most part, the country dweller, living in a kind of backwater far from the main current of Christian ministry, has to learn to rejoice in the preaching of lesser men. It has not inevitably been so, of course. Welshmen of the eighteenth and the earlier part of the nineteenth century – and they were not domiciled in great cities – had their Daniel Rowland, their Christmas Evans, and their John Elias, and from all that an Englishman can read of such ministries, it may well be supposed that they yielded 'days of heaven upon earth'. The wife-to-be of Thomas Charles, writing to her betrothed, could assure him that her visit to Llangeitho (Cardiganshire), where Rowland ministered for some fifty-five years, introduced her to what in her eyes fell little, if any, short of an apostolic ministry. Short though her visit was, it lifted her to the third heaven. Evans and Elias, too, were able to give their hearers sight after sight of 'the King in his beauty'.

No such joys have been mine. But perhaps I may mention that about 1920 I heard the famous Methodist preacher, Dinsdale T. Young, in Manchester. His message was based upon 1 Corinthians 1:23: 'We preach Christ crucified'. After castigating the Higher Critics for their evil ways, he explained the doctrine of substitution, the Just One dying for the unjust, at the same time warning any young ministers present to keep to 'Christ crucified', and not to wander off to social and other topics. He told them that if men did not like such a message, their quarrel was with the King more than with his herald. 'Get back', he urged, 'to Pauline theology'. To me it was a pleasing message.

Mr Geoffrey Williams of Evangelical Library fame in the 'twenties was the means of introducing me to the preaching of Mr Henry Popham of Eastbourne, brother of Mr J. K. Popham of Brighton. At that time Mr Williams was living at Beddington, Surrey, and certain ministers preached in his house at week-evening services. The sermons of Mr Henry Popham were singularly sweet, and I learned that, though a Strict Baptist, he was fully prepared to quote hymns outside *Gadsby*, quite a brave step to take. I found his conversation very helpful to a young man. But I saw nothing of Mr Williams' famous library, then housed at Beddington. Its move to Central London came at a much later date. The ministry of Mr J. K. Popham had made a strong appeal to my wife while in

A Circle of Friends

her 'teens. She still remembers with joy a sermon on 'access to God', the text being 'Through Him [Christ] we both have access by one Spirit unto the Father'. It was a choice discourse on the Trinity also. A second text and sermon turned her to Hebrews 3:1: 'Wherefore, holy brethren, partakers of the heavenly calling, consider the Apostle and High Priest of our profession, Christ Jesus'. Discourses of this type, severe and theological as they may appear to many, set my wife's feet firmly on the Rock. Of course she had been nurtured in the faith from the cradle; but it was Mr Popham's ministry, though only rarely heard, that confirmed all the good of parental teaching and example, and 'wrought a work on the wheels . . . a vessel as seemed good to the potter to make it'.

One principal happening in my life in the post-war period after 1945 was that I came into touch, and afterwards into fellowship, with Pastor Sidney Norton of St John's Church, Summertown, North Oxford. It would perhaps be well to mention my earliest contacts with Oxford, as my later life has already involved me in eleven years' residence in a village only twelve miles distant from that city.

I first visited Oxford in 1932, when I had been a schoolmaster for some eight years. I believed in the wisdom of attendance at occasional vacation courses such as were offered by the then Board of Education, and sometimes by universities acting independently of the State. I had already attended one such course for History teachers at Durham University in 1928, and four years later I spent a month in Oxford, taking a course of study organised by the University's Department of Education, which qualified me as a practising teacher of above seven years' experience to sit for the University's examinations at any time thereafter that I pleased. The course proved of some service to me, but as I also found that I did not care for the study of psychology and suchlike themes, I never actually took the examinations, and was further disinclined to do so when I discovered that it would not make a penny's difference to my salary.

But the month's residence gave me ample opportunity to search out the historical and cultural facets, if I may so call them, of one of England's greatest centres of learning. The library of Merton College, still preserved from mediaeval times; the Tyndale portrait in Hertford College; the Memorial to Cranmer, Latimer and Ridley, Marian martyrs, in St Giles; the cross in the tarmac of Broad Street marking the very spot where the fires that burned them were kindled; Pembroke College, where George Whitefield was an undergraduate; Christ Church, from which John Owen ruled the University for a time in the days of Oliver Cromwell; the same College and Lincoln College famous for the Wesleys, and in the case of Lincoln for the meetings of the Holy Club and the start of Methodism; the University Church in the High Street, where Cranmer made his final defence before the Romanists, renouncing their system when they were expecting him to re-embrace it, and almost running thence to the stake; Balliol College, of which John Wycliffe, the morning star of the Reformation, had at one time been Master; Jesus College, where Thomas Charles had once studied – all these and very many other links between Oxford and Christianity were of great interest to me.

In 1939 I spent a further brief period in the city with my wife and two sons (the third was not born until five years later), taking a vacation course in School Librarianship. In 1944 I attended an Inter-Varsity Fellowship course in Theology at Wadham College, Dr E. F. Kevan, whom I have previously mentioned, being also in attendance. Professor F. F. Bruce was one of the lecturers and he also gave a few introductory lessons in Biblical Hebrew to such as myself who had no previous acquaintance with the language. I ought to add that I was attracted to the course partly by the fact that, apart from Scripture itself, the textbook recommended for applicants to the course was Calvin's *Institutes*, but to my considerable disappointment, no reference to it was ever made, so far as I remember, during the entire period of instruction.

Thus by 1944 I was becoming familiar with Oxford. My second and third sons later became graduates of its University, the former in time becoming one of its Readers and taking charge of the Department of Atmospheric Physics. The latter read Engineering. And perhaps I should add that my eldest son took degrees in Physics at Manchester and London and followed a career in Meteorology. It puzzles me a little to reflect that not one of them followed my own bent academically. But much more important, by the grace of God, in late adolescence they were led to confess Christ before the world, to receive baptism in the triune Name, and to become members of Christian churches.

It was during the fortnight of the I.V.F. Course that for the first time I made contact with Mr Norton. Two friends, also attending the course, and I walked over to Summertown (about two and a half miles from the city centre) one Sunday morning, and worshipped at St John's Church. We had heard that at that church the Word of God was believed and preached in the old evangelical fashion, and such we found to be the case. But in my case at least there was the difficulty that the church was attached to the Free Church of England, and therefore its services differed in certain respects from those to which I had been accustomed.

In 1948 I had occasion to come into more personal contact with Mr Norton. My second son, at sixteen years of age, and only a few days before the new session was due to commence at the University, was awarded a scholarship by Jesus College, and as it was necessary for him to be in 'digs' for his first year on account of the lack of residential accommodation in the College, it was needful to find something that fitted his need. The official channels which I first employed yielded nothing to my satisfaction, and I turned perforce to Mr Norton. He proved most helpful and in the outcome my son was received for the first part of his first term in the house where Mr and Mrs Norton themselves were accommodated; they had rooms in the home of a lady who had been converted through Mr Norton's ministry.

As yet my son had not confessed the Lord in baptism, for my wife and I had had no wish to bring undue pressure to bear upon the consciences of our sons. In the case of each of them the crisis of conversion came to them shortly after leaving home for their university studies. My son at Oxford, wishing to join in I.V.F. activities, was faced with the problem of assenting to a certain form of words, which, as he saw and felt, could only rightly be done by a true believer in Christ and the Christian faith. At the same time we also urged upon him that a believer who had not been baptised should not sit at the table of the Lord until he had submitted to the Lord's command and the clear order of the New Testament. The crisis over, he desired baptism, and as he was in attendance at St John's Church, Mr Norton was asked to make it possible for him.

For some time, we learned, Mr Norton himself had been moving over to a Nonconformist position, and when he learned that our son desired baptism as a believer, he also felt moved to follow in the same pathway, as also, it appeared, did the Church's 'lay reader'.

When my eldest son heard of what was about to happen, he too, having experienced conversion some time previously, asked to follow in the Lord's steps on the same occasion. It so happened that St John's Church, though opened about 1930 as a Free Church of England place of worship, and following the order of a (reformed) Prayer Book, possessed a baptistry of the normal Baptist type. So far as was known, like Joseph's sepulchre, it was a place (typifying death with Christ) in which 'never man [or woman] before was laid'. A baptismal service was duly arranged, and it was my joy and privilege to travel over from North Wales, to preach the Word, and to assist the disciples to follow their Lord.

My wife and I occasionally visited Oxford thereafter, and Mr and Mrs Norton on two occasions spent holidays with us in North Wales. In the mid 'fifties Mr Iain Murray became assistant minister with Mr Norton, and at St John's the link was forged which ultimately resulted in the commencement of the *Banner of Truth* magazine, issued from the Church, which in its turn led to the founding of the Banner of Truth Trust. It was not until 1960 that I resigned my teaching post, after having spent almost a year as Acting Headmaster of my School, and not until 1962 that my wife and I came to Charlbury, Oxfordshire, to reside; our church fellowship, of course, being at St John's, Oxford, now called St John's Evangelical Free Church.

When my wife and I felt that the Lord would have us move to the Oxford area, the problem of house sale and house purchase proved a very difficult one at both ends, and caused us considerable trial and much prayer. We waited upon the Lord, and looked at various properties in the neighbourhood of Oxford, including an old vicarage (seventeenth-century) to which I was somewhat attracted. As a 'relic' of the Puritan age it appealed to me, but not at all to my wife, and it was twenty-five miles from Oxford city. We agreed to refuse it. Ultimately, when our hopes of a move had almost expired, we were led – and I use the word deliberately – to the property where we now reside, and it came to us, as a gift from the Lord. It has suited our needs admirably.

One of our problems was that of books, and their accommodation. The house at which we arrived, standing in a large garden, possessed a huge shed in which poultry were reared. Actually the whole place had once been a smallholding. The shed had doubtless once been an army hut, for it was of the precise type to which I had been accustomed in 1918 during my military career. It helped to weigh down the scale in favour of the purchase of the property. Once acquired, with the help of Mr and Mrs Norton I was able to obtain supplies of timber, by means of which I could fix up shelves and, even more important, undergird the floor, for I was certain that a considerable weight of books was more than the floor could bear. In the kind providence of God it so happened that there was a considerable work of demolition proceeding at the very time at a large store in Oxford's Cornmarket, one of the main thoroughfares of the city, and the old timber was being disposed of by the demolition contractors. I was thus able to obtain forty beams (about eight feet long), some of which I placed under the floor, while the remainder served as uprights for shelving purposes. In due time the books arrived. As many as possible I accommodated in the house, and also in a second shed which we brought with us from North Wales. Even so, there was no room to spare.

As one who has worked with the Banner of Truth Trust in an editorial capacity, the books have been invaluable to me. Only occasionally have I found it needful to consult a book in the Bodleian Library of Oxford, a fact which reminds me of a pleasantry passed by the removal contractor who brought the books from North Wales. When I remarked upon their quantity, he responded with the words, 'Oh, we are used to such a task, we moved the Bodleian'; by which he meant that when the Bodleian moved from old premises to new – the occasion when the gold key being used by King George VI to open the door on the ceremonial day broke in the lock – his was the firm that obtained the contract. I have gained greatly from having almost all the many books that I have needed close at hand. Humbly I would say that in many ways my home has virtually been a Department of the Banner of Truth Trust, at least one of its 'workshops', the entire range of editorial work in which I have been involved being carried on within its walls.

So I would record heartfelt praise to God for mercies temporal and spiritual. His ways are mercy, his acts are gracious, even if, in a certain aspect, they 'are past finding out'. Service for him is a part of blessedness. To know him, the only true God, and Jesus Christ whom he has sent, is eternal life. To live 'looking for that blessed hope, and the glorious appearing of the great God and our Saviour Jesus Christ' (*Titus 2:13*) is like 'a heaven of his surpassing love, a little new Jerusalem like to the one above'. 'Occupy till I come' is a relevant word at all times.

> *He comes, whose advent trumpet drowns*
> *   The last of time's evangels;*
> *Emmanuel crowned with many crowns,*
> *   The Lord of saints and angels:*
> *O Life, Light, Love, the great I AM,*
> *   Triune, who changest never,*
> *The throne of God and of the Lamb*
> *   Is Thine, and Thine for ever!*

10: *The Work of an Editor*

The year 1960 was the year of my retirement from the teaching profession. As mentioned in earlier chapters I became a schoolmaster in 1923 and, after holding two temporary appointments as a History master, I entered in 1925 into the appointment in Rhyl, North Wales, which I held until 1960. This third and last appointment I enjoyed to the full. To the teaching of History (after a short time, to 'A' level) I added the teaching of Scripture (also to 'A' level). In addition I was invited by successive headmasters to take a substantial part in the School's internal administration. The school library also engaged my considerable attention, as did the interests and needs of a large sixth form pursuing a variety of subjects. In my final year I found myself Acting Headmaster (an unexpected death having occurred). But at that point, for several reasons, I judged it fitting to enter upon a retirement which has endured until the present day and has provided me with 'literary work' of a Christian character for which my scholastic career had provided fitting training, and for which I have been profoundly thankful. More of this hereafter.

First, a more personal note. My wife and I had three sons who had graduated (at least, the third and youngest was about to graduate) in the sciences (principally Mathematics and Physics), the eldest in London and the two others in Oxford. So two of them were located in the Oxford area, the other in no distant place. A move for my wife and myself into the Oxford area therefore seemed desirable, and after committing the matter very definitely in prayer to the Lord we decided to make the move. One of my problems, as already mentioned, was that of books, for by 1960 I had gathered together a considerable collection relating to the Christian faith and all that pertained to it. In our North Wales home they more or less filled two large poultry sheds (for, needless to say, we did not live in a mansion) which found a place in our back garden. Not that I had any particular interest in poultry, but my wife's parents in their old age came to live with us, and the sheds had belonged to Grand-dad who had a strong interest in the feathered tribe. In North Wales, however, the sheds were given up to books, and a move southwards must include the possession of a house with a similar substantial garden able to accommodate the sheds. One chief essential was the need to be within reach of a church of God where fellowship in the things of God could be enjoyed.

Our search was somewhat protracted. Two or three journeys southwards produced nothing and we almost reached the conclusion that, after all, we must remain in North Wales. Indeed, as we set out homewards after what we had concluded would be the last visit of exploration, our hopes were little above nil. However, I suggested to my wife that, in a last venture, we should call on our homeward journey to see a property advertised for sale at the eastern end of the Cotswolds. We did so, my wife reluctantly – for she had grown weary of the search, as had I too, but more so – and before we left the area we had arranged to purchase a house with a large garden and a delightful prospect, the last house of all near the crest of a hill overlooking the valley of the River Evenlode, a tributary of the Thames. The garden already possessed an old commodious shed, dating, I imagined, from the period of the First World War, and the one shed we proposed to bring with us from home could fit well behind it (with no awkward questions proposed by the Local Authority). The house was situated on the outskirts of the village of Charlbury. It became our home for the next sixteen years. My wife died there in 1974, after which I lived alone until 1978. It was a rural retreat about sixteen or twenty miles from Oxford city centre, but our possession of a car made it easy to get to any other place in the Oxford area.

But I must explain how our Charlbury home fitted our desire to be within reach, easy reach, of a church sound in the faith. In my last chapter I explained that my wife and I had been friendly with a Mr and Mrs Sidney Norton, Mr Norton being an evangelical pastor in North Oxford (Iain Murray had become his Assistant Minister in 1955, and had remained with him until, a year later, he became Assistant to Dr Martyn Lloyd-Jones in Westminster Chapel, London). This church met our spiritual need and, thankfully, we threw in our lot with it. Mr Norton seemed glad of what help I could give him as months and years went by, and I took a share in the ministry of the Word. The New Testament draws a distinction between the *preaching* of the Word and the *teaching* of the Word, not that the two ministries are sharply distinguished as though they had no link one with the other. Indeed in many ways they are closely linked. Teaching may accompany preaching even in the same sermon. It is a poor sermon which teaches the hearer nothing at all. Some servants of the Lord seem equipped for both activities; others excel in one or the other, not in both. Suffice it to say that my previous years of service had equipped me to be teacher rather than preacher. Mr Norton, realising this after a time, seemed well content to invite me to teach the Word, that is to say, chiefly in the week-evening gathering, while he himself (or others) occupied the pulpit on the Lord's Days. Certainly I preached oft-times on the Lord's Days, but my part was, clearly, to teach rather than to preach.

Mr Norton resigned as the pastor of St John's Church, North Oxford, in 1976. He had occupied the office for about thirty-six years. Unhappily after a short time, a division of opinion was keenly felt. Certain matters of procedure, not of doctrine, were contended. In the outcome, some members (the majority) moved to an empty church building on a further side of Oxford; the minority remained in North Oxford, but by 1978 death and division had resulted in the closing of the North Oxford church, and efforts to revive it later met with no success. Sad, indeed, it is when a once lively testimony ceases to exist, and sad is the contention that leads to it.

My first wife, having been taken to be with the Lord in 1974 (as I have mentioned), the *Banner* magazine of January and February, 1975, contained my 'Tribute to a Wife and a Mother in Israel'. I lived alone in my Charlbury home for four years, but my sons judged it well to press upon my attention the desirability of obtaining a house near to one of them. I accepted their exhortation and accordingly purchased a house in the village of Begbroke, some five or six miles from the centre of Oxford city, where my second son already lived. The house was sufficiently large to contain my books, or rather, about half of them. The remainder – quite a number were not linked with religious or historical matters – I passed on to Oxfam. Those I retained I never cared to count, although friends sometimes asked me how many books I retained. My idea of numbers is 30,000, but I have never desired to know their precise number. 'Of making many books there is no end; and much study is a weariness of the flesh', runs the message

of the Preacher, and he immediately calls to the hearing of
'the whole matter' (*Eccles. 12:12–13*).

At this point of time (1978) as I waited on the Lord I
began to entertain the idea that it might be well if I
married again. The suggestion, I felt, came from no
human source. I felt that it came from the Lord. Soon my
thoughts turned to one whom I knew quite well, namely
Elsie Ash (*née* Shepherd), a widow since 1969 and wife for
twelve years previously of Raymond Ash, a lecturer in the
London Bible College. She herself had been appointed (by
Dr Ernest F. Kevan) Matron of the same College,
although formerly an employee of the (old) Board of
Education. Born in Carlisle in 1921 she had been given a
post in the Board of Education at the age of sixteen, and
thereafter lived in London. Then came the Second World
War when a section of the staff of the Board was evacuated
to North Wales. So it came about that she found herself
living in Rhyl where I myself had lived since 1925. She
knew nothing of the Lord and of his salvation, for her
family's relationship with the Church of England was
merely nominal. But it so happened that a young man in
the same office as herself, a believer linked with the so-
called Open Brethren, spoke words to her which eventu-
ally led to her conversion. As she pondered matters, being
deeply exercised, she took a lonely walk which led her to
take a rest on a hillside where sheep grazed. There the
Lord opened her heart and eyes, and she passed from
death into life, praising and blessing the name of the
Saviour of sinners.

Elsie's kind friend introduced her to what was known as
the Brigade Hall Meeting (in Rhyl), so called because it
met in premises hired from a Boys' Brigade. In the
outcome it was my joy to baptize Elsie on the confession of
her faith. My wife invited her frequently to our home, and
as days and months passed she grew rapidly in the

knowledge of the Son of God and his holy Word. She still tells me, occasionally, that, under God, I was the one who taught her 'sound doctrine'. At a later date the illness of her parents caused her to leave the Civil Service, and somewhat unexpectedly she obtained qualifications in domestic science, catering and so forth. Hence her suitability for appointment as Matron of the London Bible College at a later date. Dr Kevan tested her doctrine before he was led to recommend her appointment, and possibly it was as much for her doctrine as for more mundane qualifications that he was pleased to accept her for the post he had advertised. Later, as is now well known, she revealed her competence as a writer in the fifty chapters of a book entitled *Christian Hymn-writers* which was published by The Evangelical Press of Wales several years ago and is now in its second edition. I would mention that all the books Elsie required to consult on her chosen theme were to be found in her own home, no insubstantial help in the pursuit of knowledge, for in 1978 she and I married. She had lived for seventeen years in Reading since leaving the London Bible College.

Shortly we felt led of the Lord to leave Begbroke and live in Abingdon, some eight or ten miles south of Oxford, where was a Strict Baptist Chapel known as The Abbey Baptist Chapel. The chapel building which dated from 1832 had been built by William Tiptaft (an ex-Anglican vicar) on land he purchased which, in the sixteenth century (before the dissolution of the monasteries by King Henry VIII), had belonged to Benedictine monks. Hence the name Abbey Chapel. We knew and esteemed the Chapel's members – at least some of them – applied for membership, were accepted, and took our place with those who thus sought to follow the Lord and to 'adorn his doctrine'. Shortly, to our relief, a new pastor (Richard Chester) was appointed and we much value his ministry of the Word.

When, in 1982, the 250th Anniversary of the Chapel's founding was held, I was asked by the Oversight to write a new Life of William Tiptaft (a close friend of J. C. Philpot) which it was a pleasure to undertake. I would remark, though it may read strangely to some, that the only known portrait of Tiptaft (who died in 1864) dates from the time when he was a mere youth, studying at Cambridge University for the Anglican ministry. Thereafter, in a self-effacing way, he probably never submitted to have his portrait painted. Photography was well under way at the time of his death, but there is no known photograph of Tiptaft. His memorial is the Chapel built at his own expense in 1832.

And so Elsie and I moved to Abingdon!

*   *   *

To move 30,000 (?) books, some of them of considerable age and weight, and to find a house which would accommodate them, was a problem. We came to Abingdon to see a newly-built house, but quickly realised that its beams were by no means strong enough, nor its size (suitable for all other needs) sufficient to provide room for so many volumes. The mere transport was itself quite a problem, and not inexpensive. Faced with the problem, the writer desires to record his very sincere thanks to one of the elderly deacons. I had rendered him a very small service about ten years previously when he visited me in Charlbury to inquire whether I could help him – he was acting on behalf of friends in Horsham in Surrey – to acquire a copy of a hymn-book compiled under the title of *Hymns of Praise: A New Selection of Gospel Hymns . . . for the Use of All Spiritual Worshippers*. It had been compiled

by Edward Mote, pastor of Horsham Chapel, in 1836.
Apparently it was in regular use in his Chapel until he died
(in 1873), and possibly much later too. Mote is chiefly
remembered today as the writer of the hymn,

> *My hope is built on nothing less*
> *Than Jesus' blood and righteousness;*
> *I dare not trust the sweetest frame,*
> *But wholly lean on Jesus' Name;*
> *On Christ, the solid Rock, I stand,*
> *All other ground is sinking sand.*

Special meetings were to be held at Horsham on the
centennial anniversary of Mote's death, and an exhibition
of sundry documents, books, and so on, was linked with
the occasion. But surprisingly, nowhere could the people
of the Chapel lay hands on a copy of the hymn-book
produced by Mote. Applications to the London Evangelical Library, and similar libraries, met with no success.
How the Horsham friends came to approach my deacon-
friend of Abingdon I do not know, but his appeal to me
during a visit to my Charlbury home was the outcome. It
so happened that I possessed a copy of the Mote hymn-
book. It had belonged to my father-in-law who, as
previously mentioned, had come to live in my home, and
after his death it became mine. It contains 606 hymns, and
is well edited.

Then, later, my deacon-friend came to my rescue in
1982: 30,000 books to be moved from the house in
Begbroke to the house in Abingdon! I will call my friend
Mr W.S. for he might not wish his name to be made public
in my Reminiscences. He took upon himself the full cost
of moving the books. To begin, he brought two hundred
tea-chests (it proved that 175 were actually needed). Kind
friends from Abingdon Chapel packed the books into the
chests. A farm vehicle carried the loaded books (no light

[133]

weight!) to an empty chapel between Begbroke and
Abingdon – that which I had formerly attended – where
they could be retained for about a month until the
Abingdon house was ready to receive them. In due time
they were re-loaded and they reached their destination.
Meanwhile my friend had sent a carpenter to construct, or
reconstruct, necessary shelving in two main upstairs
rooms. Many books occupied bookcases and shelving on
the ground floor and a corridor, the house being commodious (of necessity). But to get the tea-chests, filled with
books, up the staircase (three flights, making fifty-eight
steps in all) was no light task. My friend, however, asked
his joiner to take out a first-floor window. A farm-vehicle
arrived to hoist the tea-chests to the window-ledge; thence
a small 'light railway' conveyed them to the places on the
prepared shelves which the books were to occupy. Even
so, it proved undesirable, if not quite out of the question
to accommodate in the house the books filling forty-five
tea-chests, and shelving in the double-garage adjacent to
the house met the need.

As I have said, the entire move, as far as books were
involved, cost me nothing. In what helpful ways do some
church officers use their personal resources and 'magnify
their office' (*Rom. 11:13*)! Thanks be to God!

*　　*　　*

Iain Murray has hinted that he would like me to mention
editorial work, as required of me on numerous occasions
by the Banner of Truth Trust. For some twenty-seven
years I have taken a major part in this work (enabled in the
goodness of God), despite the problems which such work
occasionally presents. Since its commencement in 1958
Banner has published not only a magazine but a considerable number of books. I should say at the outset of

comments on this part of my theme that in the decision to select and reprint this or that book from the past, I have played no part. I have been informed of decisions taken by the trustees of the Trust, and simply been invited to prepare such and such a work for reprinting. Then, too, living authors have offered their works to the Trust. A decision in favour or otherwise has been made by the trustees (though sometimes depending upon a favourable report by reviewers, including myself), and, if the omens were favourable, I (and doubtless others) have been invited to 'go through' the manuscript, eliminate any faults, and make it ready for the printer.

Some readers may be surprised to know that such editorial work is desirable, indeed essential. In the case of really old books – be they Puritan or otherwise – the old edition to be used may be most shockingly produced, as judged by today's standards. Not that this is often the case, but faults, and changes in spelling, may require correction, sentences may be so involved as to be hardly understandable, in which case they have to be broken up, and occasionally they may have to be completely rewritten. Sometimes an old book, to render it acceptable for reading by modern men, needs reshaping or abridging. Certain Puritan authors (for example, Thomas Watson writing on *Repentance* in 1667) crowd their margins with Latin quotations which, if important, have to be incorporated into the text of the work (with translations), or simply abandoned as of little if any value to today's reader. Some books, introducing obscurities, require footnotes to be introduced by the editor.

In the case of living authors great care has to be taken to avoid giving needless offence. But where obvious faults or careless slips are found by the editor – and all men are capable of them – correction has to be suggested. An editor may also find it desirable to check an author's quotations where this is possible. The author, for example, may quote poetical verses from memory and make many a slip. Some may get their facts wrong. A wrong date may be supplied. A faulty expression may need improvement. Hence an editor needs to have access to all kinds of compendiums and books of reference, if not to a man's Collected Works themselves, to facilitate such checking. Again, some of the ancients used punctuation marks in a very careless manner, and improvement is essential. Further, an old book selected for reprinting may contain sentences of tremendous length. It may be needful to break them up into their component parts, and turn, say, a twenty-line sentence into half a dozen sentences.

To check on the work of living authors is obviously more 'dangerous' than to introduce 'improvement' into the writings of long ago. An author may imagine that his production will stand all tests. Possibly he may be highly educated; his writings may be of university standard. Even so, it may be needful for the editor to supply him with a variety of suggested improvements or a hint as to the avoidance of faults. In the case of a spoken message recorded on tape and passed on to a typist, problems may also arise. A plural subject may be linked with a singular verb, or vice versa. A verifiable story taken from history or biography may be erroneously rendered. Indeed, in the worst of cases a wholesale rewriting of sentences, or even of paragraphs, may be necessary. Happy is the editor when he has to handle a manuscript produced by an expert in the literary field, whose spoken words read as well in print as when heard by the ear. The present writer can name only one living man, within his range of knowledge, whose entire work invariably reaches this high standard.

Not all speakers know how to hold forth (so to speak) in paragraphs. Correct paragraphing is essential in printed books. A paragraph should be compact, restricted to one particular aspect of the theme under discussion, of reasonable length, and closely linked, as a rule, to its predecessor and its successor. Many readers benefit by the introduction of topical headings which trace the development of a theme as it is expanded. Of course, an editor may be pedantic and his work may irritate an author. This must be avoided by all means. Common sense and good taste must be present with author and editor alike. Happy is the editor whose 'clients' have learned to trust his findings and suggestions, if wisely given.

*   *   *

One other matter I must mention as I end this further chapter of my Reminiscences. In 1963 the Lord saw good to call me to office in the testimony known as the Bible League. The League was founded in 1892, as an outcome of the Downgrade Controversy, to 'promote the reverent study of the Holy Scriptures and to resist the varied attacks made upon their Inspiration, Infallibility, and Sole Sufficiency as the Word of God'. During the first half-century of its existence its labours were widespread and varied, but by the year 1960, when the Rev J. Poole-Connor was its chief servant, its activities were almost confined to the holding of an Annual Meeting in London and the publication of the *Bible League Quarterly*. The coverage of the *Quarterly* carried the witness into various lands besides the British Isles.

In 1963 I was invited by the League's Council to become Editor of the *Quarterly*, the then Editor being Bishop D. A. Thompson (Free Church of England). I expressed my willingness to give such help as I could, but held back from accepting full editorship and suggested that for a short time I should become Joint-Editor with the Bishop. This proved a satisfactory arrangement, and in

1970 I duly became sole Editor, a post I vacated at the end of 1986, my second wife also having become Bible League Secretary in 1978, and resigning her office at the same time as myself. In all, therefore, my services to the Bible League covered a little less than twenty-five years.

The work of Editor of the *Quarterly* proved much after my own heart. It was my task to see that the magazine was well balanced as between doctrine, experience and practice, and as between theology, history and biography. I was happy to prepare a magazine which was soundly based on Holy Writ and which defended the integrity of Scripture against the multitudinous attacks launched against it in modern days. It fell to my lot also in 1980–2 (as Chairman of the League also at that time) to take the lead in the re-founding of the Bible League. Until that date it had lacked a doctrinal basis, and it seemed good at a time when we sought recognition by the Charity Commissioners to incorporate one into the League's structure. Thus was the League, in a real sense, re-founded. My task as Editor included the writing and/or acceptance of articles bearing upon present-day attacks on the Word, also upon the spiritual problems linked with the nation, the churches, and family life. But as the League's *raison d'être* (defined as above) introduced believers from various denominations into its ranks, it adopted no precise 'stance' on such matters as church membership and the interpretation of prophecy, to mention two matters only.

In recent days a generous legacy enabled the Bible League to publish a substantial book which it entitled *Truth Unchanged, Unchanging*. Its content, which it was my privilege and pleasure to edit, consisted of a selection from the best of *Quarterly* articles from 1912–62, with a smaller selection chosen from the period 1962–82 (possibly a second such book concentrating to a greater extent on the period 1962–92 will appear in the 1992 centenary year). I am happy to state that the testimony of the Bible League and the Banner of Truth Trust is virtually one testimony; at least it is one in all essential matters, and the respective coverage of the two is virtually global, although much more impressively so in the case of the Banner than of the League. May the continued blessing of the Lord rest upon both!

> *God's Word shall stand, His truth prevail,*
> *And not one jot or tittle fail.*

The Memories of a Friend
by Iain H. Murray

Such was S. M. Houghton's natural reserve that when I first urged him to write his Reminiscences there was need of some supporting argument which could add persuasion to my plea. What that argument should be was not hard to determine. Our friend's life was so intertwined with the Christian authors he knew so well that I realised he could easily write an autobiography which would give prominence to others rather than to himself. My plea, therefore, was that he should draw attention to the heritage of Christian literature and pass on to others the reasons why he so prized it. My only regret now is that he was so enthusiastic about the subject which I proposed to him as a supplementary argument that it has virtually overshadowed all else in the preceding pages. I suppose that was inevitable, for in a sense he lived to read books, teach books, treasure books, edit books and to share with others in their extensive re-publication. Summarising to me, on one occasion, his work at Rhyl Grammar School, he allowed himself to express a little pride in the fact that when he went there in 1925 the school had a library of a mere 150 volumes, housed in one small bookcase. When he left in 1960 it was one of the best school libraries in Wales. That he should have singled out this one point, passing over many other accomplishments in his long years as a schoolmaster, is certainly indicative of what lay near his heart. Nonetheless, for those of us who were privileged to know him there has to be a regret that his reminiscences scarcely mention so many other things in his life and character which we all saw and admired.

When I first met Mr Houghton (the only name by which we ever called him!) neither of us had any idea of what our meeting was going to mean; yet that afternoon in 1955 stands out in my memory. We were introduced to one another standing in the hallway of Sidney Norton's home, 162 Banbury Road, Oxford, and as we ascended the staircase – for the Nortons lived mostly on the second floor – the schoolmaster from Rhyl asked me what my personal plans were for the future. When I replied, 'To serve in the Christian ministry', there was a further question, 'And what else?' The second question took me by surprise, and I must have been at a loss for an answer. Possibly the question reflected some influence of the Christian Brethren upon his views of the ministry as a full-time calling, or perhaps it was simply that he knew that St John's Church, Summertown, was in no position to support two ministers. He did not explain. But enough was said in that first meeting to confirm what Mr Norton had told me of his shrewdness.

It was in that same year, 1955, that the *Banner of Truth* magazine started at Oxford. After the publication of the first – or possibly it was the second – issue, which I had duly edited and proof-read, there came the disturbing experience of receiving back a copy from Mr Houghton which *he* had edited and proof-read. The disparity between his effort and my own was alarming, and it might have ended these first literary endeavours there and then had it not been for the assurance of his readiness to help in the future! Thereafter, and for the next thirty years, he would see a number of items for the magazine, and all the proofs, prior to publication.

I must, however, hasten to add something about

S.M.H.'s work as a critic lest it be misunderstood. A critic he certainly was, meticulous, precise, demandingly exact. And when I add that he had been a schoolmaster for several years before I was born, it might seem that his very offer of 'assistance' was an intimidating and daunting prospect. Sometimes would-be authors, who never met him personally but whose cherished manuscripts 'suffered' from one of his critiques, conjectured that he was high-handed and authoritarian. The truth was, however, that S.M.H. combined such an unassuming meekness with his red pen that we found him the easiest of all people with whom to work. One knew that he offered criticism in order to help and he never gave it in a form which created tension if it was unacceptable. Usually, of course, he was right in proposals for changes or corrections and we young tyros wrong, but some literary questions belong to the realm of taste and judgment and there are plenty of matters in Scripture and church history over which there is room for more than one opinion. There was nothing remotely pontifical in his criticisms, and when we disagreed, as sometimes we did, his cordiality was not in the least affected. I recall on one occasion (in 1971) expressing to him in a letter a view contrary to the one which he had stated in a recent review and fearing, afterwards, that my letter to him had shown insufficient respect. When I later tendered an apology if this had been the case, his reply was characteristic: 'No, there was certainly nothing discourteous in your letter. You are fully entitled to comment favourably or adversely on a review from my pen. A reviewer, as also a writer, must expect candid comment on his work. The important thing is to maintain a good conscience before the Lord.'

Mr Houghton was not involved in the start of the Banner of Truth Trust, though indirectly, as I must explain, he played a real part. The Trust, humanly speaking, was the consequence of addresses on British

[142]

church history which I started to give at a mid-week
meeting at Westminster Chapel, London, in October
1956. My wife and I had left St John's, Oxford, at the
beginning of July 1956, and in the time that was free
before we moved to London we paid a first visit to the
Houghtons' home, Lonsdale, 21 Pendyffryn Road, Rhyl,
in early August. The five days with our new friends were
of providential help. Although I was already exploring the
riches of Christian literature, especially as it has come
down from the Reformation and Puritan periods, I had
never seen in a private home the kind of library which
filled the extensive loft of the Houghtons' bungalow and
the two former chicken sheds in the garden. One could
happily have spent months in such company! But of
immediate importance to me was the need of help in
connection with my forthcoming church history addresses. The fact was that I had never heard any lectures on
that subject and my knowledge of the whole field was very
small. Perhaps S.M.H. felt more concern over the
responsibility before me than I did, for youth usually has
the self-confidence of ignorance. It was clear enough to
him that I was a mere beginner in need of some elementary
lessons. These he readily gave and when our visit to Rhyl
was over we left enriched both with information and with
the gift of some second-hand books which were to be
invaluable to me in the addresses which lay ahead in the
next three years. Mr Houghton was my first and best
mentor in church history, and he was immeasurably more
competent to lecture on the subject than I was at that time.
Many years later he alluded to the goodness of God in his
experience and in my own with respect to the development of our initially slender gifts. Reflecting, in 1975, on
how we had both been guided in ways which we had never
anticipated in our early years, he gave me this additional
information about himself which deserves to be set down:

As a youth my heart and mind went after educational administration, a sphere into which I was placed by my father when I left school at the age of 15. I had no desire for a teaching career, and I think I was considered totally unsuited for such a career by those who knew me best. But when I had gone through University (and the Lord certainly opened the door to me for academic training, via military service – I came in for a share in an ex-service educational grant, the first ever awarded, from the British government in 1919) I found the door closed to re-entry into administration on which my heart had been set (how thankful I was later!) and I had to give thought to teaching. I praise God for *His* leading, even though it caused me great searching of heart at the time. After initial trials I began to enjoy the work of teaching, and looking back on it all, as I can now do, I admire the divine wisdom which shut me up to a teaching career. Teaching grew upon me as years went on, and the skills I learned in a grammar school flowed over, I suppose, into specifically Christian activity. But initially I dreaded to engage in the work.

The reason why some considered S.M.H. 'unsuited' to teaching was no doubt his reserved manner. He was always more 'at home' on paper than he was in any form of public speaking and he lacked some of the personality traits which are usually found in the successful communicators with young people. The casual, informal attitudes of our modern comprehensive schools would have been entirely uncongenial to him. But he possessed the vital gift essential in any true teacher, namely, a real and sympathetic interest in pupils, and as he came to know the kind of information which appeals to different age groups he was well able to awaken attention. He was ahead of his times in the emphasis he gave to the use of visual aids, and on different subjects – geographical, historical and biblical – he prepared magnificent scrolls for mural displays in his Rhyl classroom.

Sometimes, in later years, we saw how these scrolls, brought out at his home and accompanied by his questions and comments, could enthral our own children. Considering the sheer range of his academic gifts, and bearing in mind that he had to undergo many interviews before attaining to his one academic post, one cannot but be reminded of the high standard of education which was once offered in the grammar schools of England and Wales!

It often seemed to a number of us that the most influential work of Mr Houghton's life actually began on his retirement in 1960. From the start of the Banner of Truth Trust in 1957 he freely gave his advice and time as he had opportunity. His retirement coincided with the Trust's decision to produce more books – including those of modern authors – which would be typeset. The photo-printing of old titles continued and this work obviously needed no editors or proof-readers, but there was now a much larger percentage of books which did require editorial supervision prior to publication, or re-publication, and in this role Mr Houghton became, in fact if not in title, editor-in-chief. While he took directions from myself or my colleague, Erroll Hulse, with respect to the work he did for the Trust, it was for the most part we who learned from him. Every member of staff who worked with him always found it to be the happiest of relationships. For a quarter of a century, or thereabouts, after 1960 he generally gave the equivalent of a full week's work to the Trust each month, sometimes more, and to the last he was to be regularly occupied with the editorial affairs of the Trust. Our contact was chiefly by mail, as he always worked at his own home and simply kept us informed from time to time of the hours spent on different items.

After his official retirement he allowed the Trust to remunerate him – the figure was six shillings per hour! Happily that figure changed with the times, but it was always a very secondary consideration with him for he loved the work immensely, and would happily have done it freely had that been necessary.

In the last chapter of his autobiography Mr Houghton has given an idea of what is needed in an editor. He eminently embodied those necessary qualities. He had a broad general knowledge which could frequently pick up mistakes at a glance in matters biblical, historical, geographical and literary. His capacity to spot an error was remarkable and it often surprised us. On one occasion, for example, as he surveyed a manuscript prior to its publication he proposed an alteration with respect to an alleged fact. We considered this to be a slip on his part, for he seemed to have overlooked that the sentence in question was part of a quotation and the words were those of Sir Winston Churchill whose books were checked by some of the best copy-editors in Britain. But no, he had not overlooked that the point in question was within a quotation – it was simply that Churchill's statement was wrong! Of course, in all the business of checking statements for accuracy he did not rely only on his memory. He knew his way blindfold round his library and there were few points which he could not quickly turn up, either to confirm or to correct. He always wanted a statement to be checked at its *original* source, and his research frequently revealed that items of information are too often merely repeated from one author to another with a diminution of accuracy occurring in the process.

The seemingly inexhaustible patience with which he attended to detail was not simply the result of painstaking discipline, it was connected with his capacity to be interested in all knowledge of all kinds. Even at the age of eighty-six – as he was last year – there was no lessening of this feature in his make-up, as I am reminded by a detail in our correspondence. I had mentioned to him in passing that we had recently visited an out-of-the-way small country town in New South Wales named Trundle, along with one or two other places which were new to us. But an Australian country town with a name previously unknown to him was not something he could pass over. His next letter to me returned to this subject:

> I have looked up Yass and Goulburn in my atlas and found them, but Trundle I did not expect to find. It must figure only on the largest scale maps produced in Australia itself . . . I only know the word 'trundle' as a noun and a verb, but thought it might be likely that Australia's Trundle was named after some place in the Homeland. However, my large and detailed Gazetteer knows nothing of the name as far as Britain is concerned, which gave me a little surprise. It is doubtless a good old English word.

Virtually all books published by the Trust in Britain since 1960 which had to be typeset passed through Mr Houghton's hands. In the case of new titles he often saw them first in manuscript form when suggestions and improvements could be proposed to the author. From among both of these categories of books the most important were Merle d'Aubigné's *The Reformation in England* (which he edited), C. H. Spurgeon's *Autobiography*, Arnold Dallimore's definitive *Life of George Whitefield*, and John Calvin's *Sermons on Ephesians*.[1] The last-named book posed unusual problems. Our initial intention was to publish a revision of Arthur Golding's Elizabethan translation with the language modernised in

[1]Another major title which he edited but which is not yet reprinted is Thomas Hooker's classic, *The Application of Redemption*.

places and with a cross-check on the French edition of 1562. When this revision was virtually done, Mr Houghton became firmly of the opinion that much more of the Golding text needed to be set aside in favour of a new translation from the original French and so, in the early months of 1972 he immersed himself in the sixteenth-century French, rejoicing that 'this kind of work is for me a splendid first revision of the language lessons I followed fifty years ago!' By February 18, 1972, he had spent 150 hours on the *Sermons*, and by June 16, 290 hours. The volume, when published the following year, gave very little indication of the immense amount of time which S.M.H. and others had put into it.

Unquestionably the most important series of volumes upon which Mr Houghton worked through a period of eleven years were Dr Lloyd-Jones' sermons on Romans and Ephesians. He was one of a supporting trio whose team effort contributed to the preparation of these volumes. Mrs E. Burney[2] first of all transcribed the sermons from tape-recordings and then retyped the first draft after it had been revised by Dr Lloyd-Jones. At this stage, and at others, the preacher acknowledged that 'the greatest help and encouragement' came from his wife. S.M.H., the third member of the team of assistants, carefully examined the second transcription of the sermon and generally came up with so many suggested abridgements or improvements that it was a third and final draft which frequently went to the printers. Not all of his suggestions or proposed corrections were accepted, but Dr Lloyd-Jones could say in the Preface to the first volume on Romans, 'Mr. S. M. Houghton has saved me endless trouble in helping with

---

[2]A member of Westminster Chapel, London, who gave many years to securing Dr Lloyd-Jones' sermons in written form for posterity.

the preparation of the MS for publication'.[3] This same help went into another thirteen volumes on Romans and Ephesians.

★　　★　　★

I must say a few words about Mr Houghton's later homes. Of Halcyon, the 'rural retreat' just outside Charlbury, I think he was especially fond. A small house, it stood in a semi-woodland garden, sheltered by the crest of a hill behind and looking westwards across beautiful countryside. The Houghtons turned the original garage into an attractive sitting-room, while an upstairs bedroom, crammed with books, became his study. It was at a desk beside the window of this study, looking across the valley, that the largest part of his work was done for sixteen years. In winter time he commonly worked without any heat except for a hot water bottle. This was placed in the rug in a small box where he put his feet beneath his desk! But the comparative isolation of Halcyon became a drawback after the death of Miriam, his wife, in October 1974 and, in 1978, he moved to the same village as his son, Dr John Houghton, purchasing Orchard Cottage, 27 Spring Hill Road, Begbroke. We all admired his choice. It was a moderately large modern house but prettily built in the traditional cottage-style of the Cotswolds. For the first time garden sheds were no longer needed to house the books and that was just as well for they would have been out of place in the carefully laid out garden with its lawns and flower borders. The previous owner, a musician, had added a large music room to the house, with glass sliding doors facing the garden and the fields beyond where cows generally grazed. This

[3]*Romans: An Exposition of Chapters 3:20–4:25*, Banner of Truth Trust, 1970, p. xiii.

became his new 'den'. His enjoyment of Orchard Cottage would have been very incomplete had it not been that, a few months later, Elsie Ash accepted his proposal of marriage. Her coming brightened all things and turned a building into a true home.

The Houghtons moved from Begbroke to the town of Abingdon in March 1982. There was an advantage in being in a town and a chief one was the proximity of The Abbey Baptist Chapel where they were both at home. S.M.H. took a high view of the Christian's local church commitment and the Houghtons would invariably be present both for the services of the Lord's Day and at the mid-week prayer-meeting. Their new home in Abingdon (Larkhill House, 4 Godwyn Close) was a three-storied Victorian stone building, built about 1850, which had once been used by the Headmaster of the adjacent Abingdon School. Books were not, therefore, strangers within its walls, though the old house could hardly have seen such a number as required 175 tea chests for their delivery! Divided from the playing fields of the School by only a strip of lawn and a brick wall, I think Mr Houghton rather liked the sight and sounds of schoolboy activity, with the exception of the cricket balls which sometimes cleared the wall to land beneath his windows! He began one letter to me with the words:

> It is Monday (afternoon) of the 19th September . . . To my left as I look through the window (I am upstairs) boys, just returned from holidays, are running around in sports dress. It is sunny and fairly warm today, with an occasional shower . . .

Looking back on his life, he saw the hand of God in the provision and suitability of all the homes in which he had lived.

★   ★   ★

In his mid-eighties, Mr Houghton seemed as perfectly capable of the same work-load as he had carried twenty years earlier. He suffered from some deafness but he lost no powers of concentration and very little in the way of memory. Of slight and wiry build, his physique was strong and similar to that of a man who won the Sydney to Melbourne marathon race a few years ago when he had turned sixty years of age! If S.M.H. did not possess the interests he certainly enjoyed the stamina of an athlete. At the age of seventy-one he could write:

> I am conscious of living on 'borrowed time' though my health is good. I spent nine hours on Monday digging solidly (vegetable plot) which I was more or less resolved to complete in the day – and just managed to complete it as darkness fell.

Six years later, in 1977, he was well able to attack and remove a nest of wasps in his garden at Halcyon. At eighty-three he was still happy to cut a neighbour's lawn as well as his own and at eighty-six he drove the usual 180 miles from Abingdon to the holiday home of his son, John, at Abergynolwyn in Wales (ten miles inland from Cardigan Bay). At times we began to think that he might be like the great Puritan leader, Laurence Chaderton, who outlived both his contemporaries and his juniors, being over a hundred when he died! Of course, S.M.H. never made any assumption of that kind. He redeemed the time as it was given to him and kept all his affairs in good order out of consideration for others and in accord with his belief that a Christian should be always ready.

One thing which gave him particular concern with respect to his estate was his library. After not a little thought and prayer, and after discussion with friends, he was happy to decide upon giving the greater part of it to the headquarters of the Evangelical Movement of Wales at Bryntirion near Cardiff. Wales lay near his heart and, after all, most of the books had originally been obtained from various corners of the Principality.

In temperament, it must be said, our friend was very far from being a Welshman! Besides being unable to sing, he had an equable temperament and rarely revealed any emotion. He was neither elated nor depressed, and indeed he once surprised me with the quiet statement that he lacked any personal experience of depression. One example of his calmness comes to mind. On a dark winter's night while he lived at Begbroke he had to walk home from his son's house which lay on the other side of a straight main road where cars often broke the speed limit. Then in his mid-seventies, he thought nothing of the short walk in the darkness of the countryside, armed as he was with a lamp in his hand. The offer of a companion would certainly have been declined. When he was almost across the main road, which he had judged to be clear, a car at top speed passed him so closely that the light in his hand was smashed into pieces while he remained untouched. He saw it as a kind providence and quietly recrossed the road to pass on the news to his son, John, before resuming his walk!

While Mr Houghton kept very few engagements of a social nature, it would be an entire mistake to view him as a scholarly recluse. His home was a place of warm hospitality and the company of his family always gave him great pleasure. The years when he was alone at Halcyon after the death of Miriam in 1974 were difficult for him. In the course of a letter on August 1, 1975 he said to me:

> I do not know how long I may live. I continue to reside at 'Halcyon', subject to God's gracious guidance. Indeed it would be extremely difficult to move elsewhere and at the same time keep the large Library

intact for my future use. I do not know what the future holds. I am 75 years of age (76 next autumn). My health is good, but it may please the Lord to take me to Himself at any time; my 'times' are in His hand. On the other hand, even though my time is now 'borrowed' (as the saying is) He may see fit to give me another five, ten, or even twenty additional years. My father lived to the age of 96. I cannot contemplate living alone as a widower for any *very considerable* length of time, and if the Lord gives me a longer tenure of life He might provide me with a second partner . . .

This hope, as already indicated, was happily fulfilled three years later.

Something more specific needs to be said about Mr Houghton as a Christian. While there are some who might not agree – for he was strongly anti-ecumenical – I believe that he was eminently catholic in the true sense of the word. He exhibited the spirit of the chapter in *The Westminster Confession*, 'Of Communion of Saints'. Strongly Calvinistic in his convictions, he was also an admirer of John Wesley and of many other Christians of Arminian persuasion. Premillennial in his view of unfulfilled prophecy, he did not make that point an issue, though it grieved him at times that some of us were not more ardently 'looking for and hasting unto the coming of the day of God'. Only at the very end of his life was he ready to assume he would pass through death before he saw the Lord Jesus Christ. His spiritual interests were thus broad and precisely the same breadth could be seen in his library. I have beside me, as I write, a gift from him which he treasured very highly and which for long years hung close to his desk. It is a small picture frame, containing the portraits of five Christians which he had put together, also with the facsimile of a letter which reads:

Dear Sir,
    Know nothing and preach nothing but Jesus Christ.
For his sake I am your Servant.
                                    John Berridge
    Everton   April 22, 1761.

The five portraits are those of William Tyndale,
William Cowper, John Newton, Thomas Charles and
William Williams of Pantycelyn. If Spurgeon was added,
and possibly Whitefield, the list would comprise all his
favourites. The reason why he specially loved these men
was because of the fragrance of Christ about them. It
seemed to him that, like the apostle John, they knew what
it was to lean 'on Jesus' breast'.[4]

It should further be said that Mr Houghton was a
Christian who lived in profound reverence and apprecia-
tion for the Bible as the Word of God. For him the
inspiration of Scripture was far more than theory or belief;
it was the rock upon which all else depended. With John
Wesley he could say:

> I am a creature of a day, passing through life as an arrow
> through the air . . . I want to know one thing – the way
> to heaven; how to land safe on that happy shore. God
> Himself has condescended to teach the way; for this
> very end He came from heaven. He hath written it down
> in a book. O give me that book! At any price, give me
> the book of God! I have it: here is knowledge enough for
> me. Let me be *homo unius libri*.[5] Here then I am, far
> from the busy ways of men. I sit down alone: only God is
> here. In His presence I open, I read His book . . .[6]

In so far as Mr Houghton had specialist knowledge of

[4]There were also many women of whom he thought highly for the same
reason. They included Adelaide Newton, Anne Steele and Frances
Ridley Havergal.
[5]'A man of the one book.'
[6]Preface to Wesley's *Sermons on Several Occasions*.

[154]

any *one* field it could be said that his field was the text and the transmission of the English Bible. He knew it thoroughly from Wycliffe onwards – Caxton's *Golden Legend*, Tyndale's New Testament, the Bishops' Bible, the Geneva Bible (sometimes called the 'Breeches' Bible) and all else which preceded the Authorised Version of 1611 were thoroughly familiar to him. The most valuable part of his library, in financial terms, was undoubtedly his large personal collection of old Bibles. He was by no means ignorant of modern versions and he studied some of them closely. At the same time he held to the conviction that no twentieth-century version deserved to take the place of the Authorised Version, and it saddened him greatly to see that 'well of English undefiled' disparaged and set aside. He did not reject all textual criticism (as some defenders of the Authorised Version have been prone to do) but he was unconvinced of the alleged 'greater accuracy' of the eclectic Greek text underlying modern translations. 'I am all for accuracy, as you know,' he wrote to me on one occasion, 'but there are other factors, too, which come into play, and the past cannot be disregarded. Certain tendencies need to be avoided, including that which places modern university education on a pinnacle . . .'

I am not, however, wishing to emphasise here his scholarship with respect to Scripture. For more than twenty years that scholarship was clear enough for anyone to see in his work as Editor of *The Bible League Quarterly*. Our purpose is rather to say how he prized and searched the Scriptures for his own profit. To a marked degree in this respect his character matched the portrait of the godly man of Psalm 1 whose 'delight is in the law of the Lord; and in his law doth he meditate day and night'. On those occasions when he spoke of his own spiritual experience his indebtedness to the Word of God for his comfort and hope was always very evident. In one letter, written in the lonely months of bereavement following the death of Miriam, he says: 'I have been leaning hard upon the promise, "I will never leave thee nor forsake thee". I open my eyes with wonder at its antiquity and its day-to-day relevance in these "latter days". It is equivalent to living under the "shadow of the Almighty".'

He was so familiar with the text of Scripture that it often gave a tincture to his thought and words. To refer to the Bible in ordinary conversation and in an uncontrived way was far more natural to him than to most Christians. For example, in a letter written December 25, 1986, when he was more than a month past his eighty-seventh birthday, he spoke of his decision to lay down his position with the Bible League. The same decision, however, did not apply to all his labours and, conscious that his role in the Trust's work was somewhat unusual in view of his age, he was genuinely glad to note that there were biblical precedents. Who but S.M.H. could have written the following when emphasising his eagerness

> to continue my service with the B. of T. for I enjoy it much and would feel 'high and dry' if that service passed from me. I feel that I can still accomplish it satisfactorily to yourself and to the Edinburgh friends. Levite service ended, I seem to remember, at the age of 50; but Moses and Aaron endured with divine approval and aid to a much greater age, and even when Moses died, his 'natural force' (moisture) was not 'abated'.

There was nothing remotely humorous in this reference – such a use of Scripture he abhorred – it was simply that he valued the biblical indication that God has no fixed rule for the retirement age of his servants.

As a final characteristic of Mr Houghton as a Christian, mention must be made of his spiritual-mindedness and prayerfulness. While his habitual calmness was, in part, a matter of temperament, it was grace which made it such an attractive feature in his life. He knew real communion with God. He believed in the privilege of both secret and corporate prayer. His work in editing, revising or checking the writings of Christian leaders of former generations was consequently much more than a mere literary exercise. He was at one with Christians of the past. His love for their books (and their portraits) was no exercise in hagiolatry. Though they had entered into fellowship with Christ at a higher level, it was not fellowship of a different kind. He knew that the life of heaven is already begun in us, and he concurred entirely with the words of Charles Wesley:

> *Come, let us join our friends above*
> *Who have obtained the prize,*
> *And on the eagle wings of love*
> *To joys celestial rise:*
>
> *Let saints on earth unite to sing,*
> *With those to glory gone;*
> *For all the servants of our King,*
> *In earth and heaven, are one.*
>
> *One family we dwell in Him,*
> *One church above, beneath,*
> *Though now divided by the stream,*
> *The narrow stream of death;*
>
> *One army of the living God,*
> *To His command we bow;*
> *Part of His host have crossed the flood,*
> *And part are crossing now.*

There was no element of the self-conscious or the embarrassing in this spirituality. Perhaps one of the best illustrations of this occurs in his poetry. He wrote many poems, the majority for children and particularly for those of his own family circle in whom he took great

[157]

interest.[7] In these poems he intertwined everyday things which had occurred in a manner which was perfectly natural. And his verse often showed that he did not think that to be spiritual one always had to be sombre. The amusing element was also present. I am sure that his main hope was that some of these poems would be valued – perhaps many years later – for spiritual reasons by those for whom they were written. One of these poems was the result of the experience of one of our children, while on a family visit to Halcyon in 1966. Jonathan, our youngest at that time, was then a little over three years old. Not long after our arrival Mr Houghton was busy interesting the children with a number of things, including a strong, wooden letter press which could be screwed tight to hold books or other things between its two boards. Turning the handles which pressed the boards together was occupying Jonathan until S.M.H. saw the possibility of introducing the story of Paul's experience at Philippi, with Jonathan re-enacting part of the apostle's prison experience. The memorable result of this incident was later set to verse in 'Lines For Jonathan'. After four stanzas, which narrated our arrival and the children's interest in the letter press, the poem continues:

> *And then a bright idea came*
> *To Mr. Houghton, sitting low;*
> *Let Jon'than's legs,*
> *Like two straight pegs,*
> *Be put between the boards, just so.*

[7] *He kept in close touch with his three sons and their wives and followed closely all the news of his eight grandchildren. In the summer of 1984 he went to Cambridge to see one of his granddaughters receive her medical degree, and to London to be at the wedding of a grandson at St Helen's, Bishopsgate. The next year he was at the wedding of another granddaughter at Jesus College, Oxford, and he wrote to us, with special pleasure, of the baptism of twelve-year-old Simon Houghton (son of Paul and Frances). The birth of Nicholas James Houghton, a first great-grandchild, in the spring of 1986 was another joy to him.*

No sooner was it said than done;
The screw was turned, as pris'ner sat;
  No cause for fear
  As boards drew near,
Yet little heart went pit-a-pat.

To stocks the press was now compared;
See Paul and Silas, scourged and sore;
  In prison they
  Philippi way;
Read Book of Acts, sixteen-two-four.

But O, mid tears, our pent-up friend
Yielded to fear – a piteous sight –
  Features were glum,
  Release must come;
No stocks for him could yield delight.

So out he came, free once again;
Comfort returned with love's caress.
  Avoid we must
  (and shall, we trust)
All such too fearful playfulness.

But O may we, whene'er we find
Our feet held fast in life's stern press,
  Raise then our cry
  To God on high,
And find relief in our distress.

For several days after this visit to Halcyon Jonathan was often heard to say, 'Mr Houghton put me in the stocks', and I think it was our host's penitence over misjudging, in this case, the use of a visual aid, which led to the poem in twelve stanzas! On our annual visit, the following year, we all arrived sad and somewhat tearful. In the course of our drive from London the family pet, a golden cocker spaniel puppy, had been run over when we had stopped briefly beside a country road outside Henley. The dog had to be left at a local vet with no promise that we would see her alive on our return journey that evening. The grief and subsequent thankfulness at the dog's surprising survival were duly put to verse in a poem which we received a few days later. One of his best poems, written while teaching at Rhyl, is included below.[8]

These poems reveal not only a sympathy and playfulness which belies the impression which S.M.H. sometimes gave to those who did not know him, but they show how readily he could see all things in a spiritual light.

*   *   *

I last saw my friend in April 1987, before I had to return to Australia. The previous month it had been diagnosed that he was suffering from cancer and, although he was not apparently told, his life-expectancy was now very short. To him the lack of information made no difference for he could truly say with Richard Baxter,

> *Lord it belongs not to my care*
> *Whether I die or live . . .*

In the previous two years he had accomplished some of his most valuable work for the Trust but, remarkably (for despite his speed in working there had often been a backlog awaiting his attention), there was nothing outstanding at this time. He had even gone over all the two-thirds of the chapters in my second volume of the *Life of Dr Martyn Lloyd-Jones* which were written.

The last sight I have of him in my mind is standing in

[8]See pp.166–67

front of his long-cherished volumes of Spurgeon's *Metro-politan Tabernacle Pulpit*, in his upstairs study at Larkhill House – the room which overlooked the Abingdon School playing-fields. His subject of conversation for a few moments was the wonder of the coming gathering of the church of all the ages in glory, and of our own meeting with those of the past from whose witness we have gained so much. Then, with a gesture towards the shelves behind him, he bore testimony to all that those sermons continued to mean to him and of how he admired the fullness and balance of Spurgeon's ministry.

After April he continued to work at a number of small items over which we sought his advice, and until nearly a week before his death – except for going to bed a few hours earlier in the evening – his routine was little affected by his illness. On June 10 he wrote us of his approval of a critique of the N.I.V. which was in preparation for publication, with a short reference to his health:

> I am getting weaker, for I eat very little. But the Lord is good and kind and merciful. I am specially blessed by the words found in Romans 14: 'Whether we live, we live unto the Lord; and whether we die, we die unto the Lord: whether we live, therefore, or die, we are the Lord's'.

I read these words in Australia, signed with his usual, 'Much love in the Lord', about the very day in which he peacefully finished his course. To me, at least, it meant something that the date was June 19, Spurgeon's birthday. 'Other men', said our Lord Jesus Christ, 'laboured, and ye are entered into their labours' (*John 4:38*). Days of birth and of decease may mean little to the world, but a Christian sees them as all part of one on-going kingdom of Christ. What Sidney Houghton richly received he had passed on. And he rejoiced in the knowledge that finally

[161]

the handing down of the truth is not man's work at all. As one generation passes and another comes, the church will not lack faithful servants until the day of Christ. As for what he was personally, we do not doubt that God's words in Malachi 2:5–6 could truly be his epitaph:

My covenant was with him of life and peace; and I gave them to him for the fear wherewith he feared me, and was afraid before my name. The law of truth was in his mouth, and iniquity was not found in his lips: he walked with me in peace and equity . . .

Or, more briefly, in the words of Genesis 5:24,

S.M.H. 'walked with God: and he was not; for God took him'.

The Last Days of S. M. Houghton
by Richard Chester[1]

In March of this year [1987] Mr Houghton went to his doctor because of some discomfort he was experiencing in his throat. Cancer was diagnosed. Just a few days before this and completely unaware of his planned visit to the doctor I had read with him Psalm 112. Verse 7 of that psalm proved particularly appropriate. It speaks of the godly man who 'shall not be afraid of evil tidings: his heart is fixed, trusting in the Lord'. That so aptly described Mr Houghton during the last weeks of his life as he underwent radio-therapy treatment, finally taking to his bed only a few days before he died. His heart was fixed, trusting in the Lord. He was quite certain the cancer was from the Lord and never once complained.

The last time he attended chapel was the Sunday morning of May 31 when I spoke on Psalm 118 verse 24: 'This is the day which the Lord hath made; we will rejoice and be glad in it'. We considered the New Testament use of that passage which speaks so clearly of the gospel day and the stone which had become the headstone of the corner. At the door afterwards he shared with me his joy in the glory of the gospel of Christ and the truths of our final hymn, 'Sovereign grace o'er sin abounding'.

[1]Pastor of The Abbey Baptist Church, Abingdon, where Mr Houghton was in membership. This narrative is reprinted by courtesy of the *Bible League Quarterly* where it first appeared in the October – December issue, 1987.

[163]

On the Wednesday following I visited him at his home where he had been working at his desk all morning. He never studied or even read a book in an easy chair – always at his desk. He handed me a copy of Spurgeon's *Lectures to My Students* which he had purchased for the church library. He had dipped into it and much to his annoyance had found a printing error. He told me the page number and line – and sure enough it was corrected at that point! By this time he had no desire for food and told me he was dying of the cancer but was perfectly at rest in the matter. The next moment he was asking after my unconverted daughter and the affairs of the church. We read John 10:1–10. It was about this time that Mervyn Barter of the Banner of Truth visited him and was greeted with the question, 'Have you brought me any work?'

On Tuesday June 9 he was in bed when I visited. A volume of Spurgeon's Sermons (for 1885) lay open by his side. He had just read one with some difficulty. He loved these sermons above anything else, except his Bible; and he felt the Banner of Truth reprints covered Spurgeon at the zenith of his power. He quoted a verse from Watts' hymn, 'There is a land of pure delight':

> *But timorous mortals start, and shrink*
> *To cross the narrow sea;*
> *And linger shivering on the brink*
> *And fear to launch away.*

'I know nothing of that', he said firmly. Frequently during the visits he commented on the fact that 'in a moment he would be in the presence of Christ'. His face shone as he spoke. That is what death meant to him. We spoke that day of the Christian's great inheritance – incorruptible, undefiled and that fadeth not away. I reminded him that the three things that spoil life now, death, sin and change will no longer affect us then. 'Yes,' he said, 'but changelessness is not the same as tiresome-ness!' I read Psalm 107:1–8 which he recited with me from memory.

On his final Sunday on earth two of the deacons from the church stayed with him, one in the morning and one in the evening. In the morning he and the deacon had a full session of hymns, prayer, reading and, yes, a sermon read from Spurgeon! Two days before he died he spoke again with me of his absolute assurance of glory. I read from 2 Peter 1 on the abundant entrance into the everlasting kingdom of our Lord and Saviour Jesus Christ. He, however, fastened on to the previous verse, 'give diligence to make your calling and election sure'. He expressed gratitude to God that from the beginning of his Christian experience he had been brought to love 'the doctrines of grace'. He could not understand how anyone could deny them. That afternoon we spoke together of Christ's appearing, even though he knew that he would die before the Lord came again. This was the last time I saw him in a conscious state. A lady who visited him late that day told me that he simply pointed his finger heavenwards.

He lapsed the next day into semi-consciousness though, characteristically, even in that state was asking, 'Has the post been?' (His letters were always answered by return of post.) The following day, Friday June 19, I called early in the morning. He was unconscious and breathing heavily but regularly. At ten minutes past ten he breathed his last and Sidney Houghton is now 'for ever with the Lord'.

To The Girl Who Smiled
by Invigilator (S.M.H.)

'Twas Latin Exam; the quad doors were wide open;
The time of two-thirty appeared on the clocks;
So deep was the silence I almost caught echoes
Of the love-sighs Sweet Williams exhaled to the Phlox.

My eye roved around as I watched girls performing,
Their pens moving fast as distinction they sought,
When I noticed a maid look hard at her paper,
And what she did next gave me subject for thought.

SHE SMILED TO HERSELF; what thoughts were a-
    stirring?
What pleased her so much when all brows were tight knit?
Was it Cicero's quips that tickled the fancy?
Or was it pure joy in an answer she'd writ?

Perchance it was Caesar, but he has no humour;
Mayhap it was Virgil with rich country airs;
Perhaps it was Horace the maiden befriended,
And eased for a moment a candidate's cares.

O fons Bandusiae splendidior vitro;
Was it this which called forth the facial beam?
Fies nobilium tu quoque fontium;
Did the lilt of the lines help to fashion the gleam?

[166]

The sparrows outside might contribute their twitters,
The sunshine might blaze, for better, for worse,
But a smile such as this, unexpected and precious,
Was surely most fitting t'elicit my verse.

What caused it I know not, nor need I pursue it;
A smile's but a fleeting and soon-forgot thing,
But mem'ry will cherish in years not yet dawning
That the candidate found in the desert a spring.

Let Caesar and Virgil and Horace all perish,
Their lines, though immortal, are pleasing to few,
But a smile from a maid on such an occasion
Lives on in my mind delightfully new.

But who was the maiden? Forsake such a query;
The secret lies hid in the mind of but one;
Concealed let it stay so that each who took Latin
May surmise it was she I dilate thus upon.

S. M. Houghton's Writings

William Tyndale: His Life and Times, Sovereign Grace
Union, 1927, reprinted 1986, Focus Christian Ministries Trust, 6 Orchard Rd., Lewes, East Sussex, pp.
16.

The Banner of Truth. For articles by Mr Houghton see
published Index for the years 1955–85.

The Bible League Quarterly. Many articles from Mr
Houghton appeared in the *Quarterly* from 1963
onwards.

Tourist in Israel, Banner of Truth Trust, 1968, pp. 220.

Isaac Watts, The Annual Lecture of the Evangelical
Library, London, 1974, pp. 44.

Sketches From Church History, An Illustrated Account of
20 Centuries of Christ's Power, Banner of Truth
Trust, 1980, pp. 255.

*Truth Unchanged, Unchanging, A Selection of Articles from
The Bible League Quarterly* 1912–82 (Edited), The
Bible League, 1984, pp. 503. This volume contains
several of the editor's own articles.

The Life of William Tiptaft, The Abbey Baptist Church,
Abingdon, 1982, pp. 38.

The Bible Witness Hymnal (Edited), The Cotswold Bible
Witness, a selection of 209 hymns, 1972.

Index